Peter is International Director for Tearfund. He previously worked for 15 years for the Department for International Development of the UK government. Peter and his wife Stella are members of Bedford Hill Baptist Church in South London.

POOR NO MORE

Be part of a miracle

PETER GRANT

MONARCH
BOOKS

Oxford, UK & Grand Rapids, Michigan, USA

First published in the UK in 2008 by Monarch Books
(a publishing imprint of Lion Hudson plc),
Wilkinson House, Jordan Hill Road, Oxford OX2 8DR
Tel: +44 (0) 1865 302750   Fax: +44 (0) 1865 302757
monarch@lionhudson.com
www.lionhudson.com

Distributed by:
UK: Marston Book Services Ltd, PO Box 269,Abingdon, Oxon OX14 4YN.
USA: Kregel Publications, PO Box 2607, Grand Rapids, Michigan 49501.

ISBN: 978-1-85424-840-4 (UK)
ISBN: 978-0-8254-6281-8 (USA)

Cover photo: A young boy from the remote Quechua village of Guitarrani. Photo: Richard Hanson/Tearfund

This book has been printed on paper and board independently certified as having been produced from sustainable forests.

British Library Cataloguing Data
A catalogue record for this book is available from the British Library.

Printed in Malta by Gutenberg Press.

Contents

For Stella, Lucy and Matthew,
whose faith, love and encouragement
mean so much to me.

Acknowledgments

Carolyn Scriven, a special friend of all our family, has played a key role in seeing this book completed through her encouragement and guidance. I am grateful to my family and friends who have commented on drafts of the full text, including Stella Grant, Lucy Grant, Matthew Grant, Rachel Carnegie, David McIlroy, Paul Cook, Val Stevens, Steve Bradbury and Les Ball. My thanks go to Sarah and James Jones for writing the foreword; and to friends at Bedford Hill Baptist Church for their prayers and support. An excellent consultation of the Micah Network on the Church and Integral Mission took place while I was writing this book, and I am grateful to Steve Bradbury, René Padilla and Melba Maggay for their challenge to my complacency.

I joined Tearfund in 2005, after fifteen years of working for the UK Government's Department for International Development. I have learned a huge amount from colleagues in both organizations. Tearfund is passionate about following Christ, and inspired by the vision of a global movement of local churches bringing justice and transformation within poor communities. This book seeks to reflect this energy and commitment. I am privileged to be part of leadership teams at both church and work that are characterized by integrity, openness and mutual support.

Thank you to those at Tearfund who have commented on chapters in draft and provided other insights, including Andy Atkins, Paul Brigham, Paul Cook, Bethan Davies, David

Deakin, Graham Fairbairn, Matthew Frost, Mari Griffith, Jenny Grove, Mike Hollow, Sara Kandiah, Andrew McCracken, Ben Niblett, Tulo Raistrick, Rachel Roach, David Smith, Gary Swart, Sue Towler, Laura Webster, David Westlake and Jon Yates. Special thanks to Dewi Hughes for theological comments and great discussions. The responsibility for the content is mine, and it does not necessarily represent Tearfund policy. All the incidents described in this book are factual, but some names have been changed to preserve anonymity.

I am conscious of my hypocrisy in writing a book like this. I am not doing all the things that I recommend. But I am part of a group of people at Tearfund who realize increasingly that addressing global poverty means changing ourselves. We are all journeying together as the people of God as we seek to deepen our discipleship. God has moved me on during the writing of this book. I still have a long way to go.

One of the biggest struggles was choosing a title. To Amy and Michaila, let me say your suggestions were definitely the best, even if I couldn't use them.

Foreword
by Sarah Jones and James Jones,
Bishop of Liverpool

Sarah was one of the original four people who started Tearfund; James is one of Tearfund's Vice Presidents.

This book reads like a letter from Peter Grant. He writes unashamedly to get you involved. It's a conversation of convictions as each page urgently invites you to sign up to be part of a miracle to eradicate poverty in the name of Christ.

The world is awash with statistics about global poverty and environmental degradation, so much so that you can feel overwhelmed and paralysed. You know that you should do something but the task feels so enormous that it's impossible to know where and how to begin. What you need is a friend to guide you. You'll find him in these pages!

Peter is an experienced sherpa who has worked at a senior level in Government and International Development. He knows the complexities and is a skilful negotiator who can cut through the thicket of graphs, charts and tables. Through his work with Tearfund he's able to illustrate the text with cameos from around the world that make the figures come alive. Above all he applies everything to the writ of Scripture which is the greatest authority in guiding us on what to believe and how to behave.

Peter shows on page after page the inextricable link between believing in a God of justice and behaving justly. He shows that you cannot claim to be at one with the God of justice without at the same time being caught up in the divine dynamic of acting justly, loving mercy and walking humbly with God. Peter powerfully illustrates how the doctrine of justification by faith is the foundation of Christian ethics which call every follower of Jesus to a life of justice and compassion.

Peter has operated on the inside of the big organizations and understands how the big players operate in today's world. DFID, the World Bank and International NGOs have become very sophisticated operators. Peter understands the structures of these organizations, their strengths and weaknesses. But he also knows how the individual exercises great power as both citizen and consumer. He shows how the Davids of this world can make an impact on the Goliaths. It is why he quotes Bill Hybels' statement that 'the local church is the hope of the world'. Oceans are filled by mighty rivers as well as by tiny drops of rain. If we Christians in our small communities took seriously the message of the Bible, we would be transformed and could transform the world.

When we give, that is when we behave most like God. In his love God gives not just the world but his very self. Loving and giving go together. When we give of ourselves for the sake of poor people, we are following in the footprints of Jesus.

By the time you have finished this book you will not be able to say, 'Well, I don't know what to do.' This book amounts to a rule of life. It will also change your life.

CHAPTER 1

A Call to Action

God wants people to be free from poverty. He is looking for an end to the oppression and misery that it brings, and for people to enjoy fullness of life, to be *poor no more*. His plan involves you and your church. In fact it requires a global movement of Christians and local churches passionately committed to seeing the lives of poor people transformed. You can be part of this miracle.

This book is aimed at Christians who want to make a difference. It is a call to exercise your faith – learning to see people with God's eyes, to love them as he does and then to act – trusting that as you step out, and despite your weakness, God will do a miracle and multiply your efforts.

As you get involved, you will discover that God also wants to transform you. As a reader of this book, you are rich in global terms. If global poverty is to be reduced, then you need to do something about it. But God also wants to take away your own spiritual poverty; whether a poverty of compassion, or relationships, or of concern for others. By committing yourself to the needs of poor people, you too can be *poor no more*.

It is unacceptable that there is extreme poverty in our world – unacceptable because of the suffering that it brings to millions of people, and unacceptable because it could be eliminated. Jesus warned the leaders of his day that they were neglecting 'the more important matters of the law – justice, mercy and faithfulness' (Matthew 23:23). We must seek to share God's priorities. He cares passionately about poor people and commands us to respond to the spiritual and physical needs of the world.

Perhaps for the first time in history, a substantial reduction in extreme poverty, some would even say its eradication, is possible in our generation. Just imagine an end to the poverty that leads to 30,000 children dying needlessly every day. Such hope is desperately needed by the unprotected and silent victims of preventable diseases such as malaria and cholera, by the children who dodge between cars in the megacities of Asia to sell newspapers, and by the women facing rape and torture in Darfur.

Be encouraged. By reading this book you are demonstrating a desire to be involved, and there are many things that you can do to have a significant positive impact. You can help to free people from poverty.

We are all connected

We are all strongly connected to poor people, even those in the remotest parts of the world. I like eating green beans, but I used to be less keen. 'Eat your vegetables – think of the starving children in Africa,' echoes a voice from my childhood. I never understood how eating my beans could make any difference to people on the other side of the world. Yet today, we affect people everywhere through our actions, both positive and negative. We are all connected.

We are connected through trade and investment. A generation ago my green beans would probably have been grown close to home. Now they come from Kenya, where agricultural workers depend for their livelihoods on my purchases. Low prices for our clothes are dependent on low wages overseas. Our pensions are invested in companies that operate globally, affecting employment and working conditions.

We are connected through our neighbours. My wife,

Stella, and I live in Streatham in South London. The last few years have seen the establishment of a Somali community near us, while our neighbours come from Malawi on one side and Pakistan on the other. Your neighbourhood may not be so diverse, but we are all experiencing the impact of globalization, bringing new cultures, food and experiences into our societies.

We are connected through the environment. We can no longer escape the reality that we live on a single, shared planet. Climate change demonstrates this dramatically. Our carbon emissions are going to contribute to the flooding of Bangladesh. If my green beans come by air, then they too are adding to global warming. Should I buy them to encourage economic growth in Kenya, or avoid them to save the environment?

We are connected through the Internet, and can access information instantly about any country in the world. We are connected through travel and the media. Our holidays become more and more exotic, and provide the opportunity to visit poorer countries. But is our tourism improving the lives of poor people? And what about the greenhouse gases emitted by our flights? Should we give up low-cost air travel? Is this a problem for governments to solve, or do we have a personal responsibility?

We are particularly connected through the church. As the body of Christ, we rejoice with those who are rejoicing, and hurt with those who are hurting. Poverty is not about 'them and us'. We are all called to express solidarity with each other as we participate in God's mission in the world. Churches in poor communities are using their resources to meet the needs of their own communities, and we can support them within a genuine two-way partnership, as part of a global movement sharing spiritual and material blessings.

What impact are you having?

With all these connections, how can you have a positive impact on world poverty? How can you make life better for farmers in Africa struggling to feed their families as global cotton and coffee prices fluctuate wildly? Or for people like the wife of a good friend of mine in Malawi who had to give birth by the side of the road because they couldn't afford a taxi to get her to the hospital in time?

Jesus gives us personal responsibility for people everywhere. His command to love our neighbour, and the parable of the good Samaritan, remove all the boundaries that we would like to place on our own accountability. This book is a chance to assess how you affect the poorest people on earth, and to take action so that you have a more positive impact in the future. This will often be through very simple choices about priorities, relationships and your use of money and time.

The madness of materialism and the perversion of power

If we care about reducing poverty, we will need to confront the realities of the world in which we live. Let me highlight two themes.

The first I call the 'madness of materialism': the mistaken belief that consumption will bring happiness. Consumerism is the dominant global religion of our age. As we spend more and more in the West, there are few signs of growing joy and contentment, and considerable evidence that the excessive working hours, environmental degradation and indebtedness that are associated with consumerism have reduced the quality of our lives. We get caught up with our own comfort and forget about poor people. We spend twice as much on ice cream in Europe than would be required to get the remaining 100 million children currently out of school into primary education.[1.1] We need to wake both ourselves and others up to the way in which materialism has come to dominate our lives and to squeeze out both God and our concern for poor people.

The second is the 'perversion of power' that we see in the economic and political systems of which we are all a part. There are many positive political developments and initiatives in our world, but we accept too easily a world where rich countries spend about eleven times as much on arms as we do on global poverty reduction.[1.2] The Bible warns repeatedly against the dangers of wealth and the oppression of the poor by the rich. We live in a world that idolizes the rich and famous; a world in which our stock markets pressurize senior executives to maximize profits at the expense of jobs, the environment and even their own health; and a world in which rich countries subsidize food exports in a way that makes it impossible for poor farmers to sustain their livelihoods. The Bible calls upon us to take a stand for justice.

Add these two together and you have the recipe for much of the inequality that we see in the world today, and for the sadness of unfulfilled lives in both rich and poor countries. Fighting against poverty will mean taking a stand against some of the dominant forces of our generation. God wants us to be prophetic by showing this generation that there is a different way to live.

What does poverty reduction require?

Poverty reduction requires both rich and poor people to be transformed. We all need to experience reconciliation with God, with other people and with our environment. Rich people need to escape from materialism and selfishness. Poor people need an end to oppression, and access to justice, healthcare, education and job opportunities.

Such changes require action by you and the church.

There are over 2 billion Christians worldwide. If a significant proportion of churches could be mobilized into a movement of people loving and serving their communities, then the world would be changed. Bill Hybels has described the local church as 'the hope of the world'.[13] That hope is seen when Christians love their neighbours through words *and* practical deeds of service; telling the good news about Jesus, while also addressing economic poverty and injustice. There are enough resources, even within the incomes of existing Christians, to finance the action that is needed. It's a question of priorities.

Home is where you start from

If you want to love and change the world, you have to start from home. As a teenager, I lived in the Sparkhill district of Birmingham. Our home was on the boundary of the white and Asian communities. I lived close to people I did not know, and felt vaguely apprehensive towards them. Walking around our neighbourhood, I passed sweet shops I never visited, and newspapers I could not understand. I was in the midst of other communities, but unable to take the final step that would have allowed me to make friends. I want to learn from this experience, and to encourage you to make the most of the opportunities that you have to reach out and form friendships across such boundaries.

Returning to Birmingham now, I see a vibrant community in Sparkhill. Many families are Muslims of Pakistani origin from Kashmir. The sweets turn out to be delicious, even if the newspapers in Urdu remain incomprehensible. Integration and political voice have improved in many ways over the past generation, but the 'war on terror', the London bombings and the war in Iraq have led to tensions and uncertainty.

The Kashmir earthquake of 2005 provided an opportunity for the community in Sparkhill to strengthen links with Pakistan through the provision of emergency assistance to earthquake victims. In May 2006 I travelled to Pakistan with Tearfund and saw the communities from which the parents of my neighbours in Birmingham had come. I saw the Tearfund response to the Kashmir earthquake in a town called Bagh; Christians demonstrating the love of Christ to communities devastated by the destruction of their homes and the death of their families. I got some sense of the culture of a people who live in remote and hostile mountain conditions, practise warm hospitality and have suffered for a generation from the tensions of the hostility between Pakistan and India. I saw new piped-water schemes, sat with the men in a village health-education class and heard how improved house design could help, at low cost, to make new homes more resistant to future earthquakes.

On my return, and most amazingly of all, I discovered that Tearfund supports a project in the very road in which I grew up. The Springfield project is based at St Christopher's parish church. It grew out a vision of volunteers within the church to support families in the area and now runs a parent-and-toddler group, a pre-school nursery and an activity club for older children. Through the project, the church has formed deep relationships with the Kashmiri community and the local mosque, which is also at the bottom of my road. The project has shown in practical ways how the gospel can be as relevant to those in need in Birmingham as in Bagh. When I visited, there was a bouncy castle inside the church and various groups of young children walking around the buildings, bubbling with excitement as they waited their turn. The multi-ethnic congregation has supported a project that benefits local children and demonstrates God's love across the boundaries.

You can make a difference, particularly with others

Why should you bother? Can one person really make a difference? What you do directly will only have a small impact on global problems, but it will have some effect. You are responsible to use the gifts and opportunities that you have, and not those that you don't. But even more significant is the challenge that your life can be to others. As part of a movement of Christians you can make a huge difference through your church and in your society. This movement needs pioneers. Never underestimate the impact of your life on others, particularly when you seek to live differently from your prevailing culture.

You are accountable to God to discover what he wants from you and then to do it. That will mean acting courageously. God calls on you to share his passion for justice. As you reflect on the sacrifice of Jesus for you and understand the needs of those who are poor, then you must act. 'If any one of you has material possessions and sees a brother or sister in need but has no pity on them, how can the love of God be in you? ... let us not love with words ... but with actions and in truth' (1 John 3:17–18).

A call to action

You only have one life. How are you going to spend it? How can you make the biggest difference for good? You can't do everything, but bombarded by so much information and challenge, it's easy to do nothing. You need to focus your attention on a specific group of people, countries and issues where you are likely to have maximum impact. You need to think about the consequences of how you spend and save your resources. You need to develop good habits in prayer and giving, but also to stretch your creativity to the limits to campaign, to write and to use the arts and media to raise awareness. In fact almost any gift you have can be used in overcoming poverty.

Your choices matter for AIDS orphans in Zambia struggling to bring up their younger brothers and sisters, for mothers in Bangladesh dying in childbirth and for farmers in Burkina Faso seeing their life savings disappear as animals die in widespread droughts. The biblical vision is not that everyone should have a European or North American standard of living, but that there should be enough for all, based on a generous redistribution of resources. Enough for everyone to have basic education and healthcare, and to enjoy safety and dignity in a community where people can share and celebrate together. Poverty denies people these basic elements of a fulfilled life.

Being part of a miracle

What is a miracle? It is God demonstrating his authority and power in an extraordinary way. A miracle is a visible sign of his presence, and the reality of his kingdom. Poverty reduction requires two main miracles. The first is the change required in the hearts of rich people if we are to give up some of our privileges. The second is the transformation in the lives of people who move from poverty to fullness of life in all its dimensions. Poverty reduction will require spiritual battles to be won, and prayers to be answered. It will require a miracle that goes beyond our human experience or resources. Let's be part of this miracle.

This book is a call to adventure. Following Jesus and loving people is what you were made for. The cultures of the world are so diverse and there is so much to learn and enjoy. My aim is to give you new eyes and a new vision for your road, your local community and the world. I want to inspire you to care and to act. The only requirements are love and a willingness to change your lifestyle, to go those final few yards to interact with people from other cultures. No age restrictions and no special qualifications are required. We are all much closer than we think.

Outline of the book

Part 1 (chapters 2 to 5) brings together some facts about global poverty, an analysis of its causes, and biblical teaching on our responsibility. It helps you to understand what action is required and by whom. Part 2 (chapters 6 and 7) allows you to reflect on your current impact through your use of time, relationships and money, and then to develop your priorities for prayer and action. Part 3 (chapters 8 to 16) sets out a nine-point action plan for positive change. In each of these chapters I have included a section on biblical teaching, ideas for action and references to useful websites. Chapter 17 brings it all together with a call for you to take forward your own personal plan of action.

So let's set out on the adventure...

PART 1

The Causes and Cures of Poverty

CHAPTER 2

Why Should We Get Involved?

*Hunger, disease, the waste of lives that is extreme poverty
are an affront to all of us…we could be the first generation
to outlaw the kind of extreme, stupid poverty that sees a
child die of hunger in a world of plenty…*

Bono (in his foreword to *The End of Poverty* by Jeffrey Sachs)

How could we let our hearts be so cold?

Kay Warren (Saddleback Church, California,
HIV and AIDS conference, November 2006)

We need people who force us to face the truth. In conversation
with the American pastor Bill Hybels in 2006,[2.1] Bono laid out
his passion for poor people and his frustration with the
church. He noted the judgmental attitudes that so often char-
acterize Christians, but also the remarkable potential for the
church to lead the fight against poverty. Bono highlights grace
as the key change that Jesus brought to human history. As
Christians, we no longer get what we deserve, but we benefit
from God's gift. No one but Jesus offers this unconditional love
and acceptance. This in turn creates the possibility for
Christians to live in the service of others. Jesus gave up the
riches of heaven to share the poverty of earth. We are called not
to enrich ourselves, but to use all that we have to serve others.

Most of us know the truth of Bono's words and the reality of global poverty, but our hearts are cold. Kay Warren from
Saddleback Church has been brutally honest in talking about
the hardness of her heart when confronted initially by AIDS.
She describes her journey through brokenness and tears to

stand with poor and marginalized people. She has made friends with people living with HIV, volunteered in programmes to serve poor people, spoken out on HIV issues within the church and demonstrated the impact that one woman, on fire for God, can have.

I know that my heart needs to be softened to respond to the needs of the world. It helps to learn about other people's journeys. Hearing Kay Warren speak inspired me to want to change. Each of us needs to go on a journey with God if we are to escape selfishness and become part of God's miracle. This chapter explains some of the reasons why you should be on this journey.

God's command requires it

God's desire is that there should be no poor people. No poor people in the church and no poor people in the world. I state this bluntly because we have focused too much on the persistence of poverty, rather than on God's desire to see it ended, and our responsibility to make it happen. God wants to see justice, and this requires that rich people repent and change. Our goal should be the elimination of poverty, nothing less.

There are two foundational statements about poverty in Deuteronomy 15:

- Verse 11: 'there will always be poor people in the land'.
- Verse 4: 'there need be no poor people among you'.

Jesus quoted the first of these in Matthew 26:11, when others were challenging the use of money for perfume to anoint him, given the needs of poor people. Poverty will persist until the end of time. But that is not to say it is acceptable. The early church in Jerusalem showed what was possible: '...there were no needy persons among them' (Acts 4:34). Jesus was not giving us an excuse for doing nothing just because poverty will always be here.

It's a bit like salvation. 1 Timothy 2:4 states that God 'wants all people to be saved'. The Bible recognizes that there will be many people who will reject God, but we pray with passion for people to be saved, because we are confident that this is God's desire. Let's also be passionate about praying and working for the elimination of poverty.

God said that there need be no poverty in ancient Israel because he was giving them the resources to provide adequately for everyone, and his law to guide them into love and generosity. We have God's Holy Spirit within us and hugely greater resources than Israel enjoyed. What is preventing us from working to end global poverty?

There are specific places in the Bible where God commands us to:

- seek justice (Isaiah 1:17);
- feed the hungry, even if he or she is our enemy (Romans 12:20);
- engage in radical redistribution of wealth through our personal giving (2 Corinthians 8:13–14); and
- live a lifestyle that glorifies God and serves poor people (Isaiah 58).

Micah 6:8 sums it up: 'What does the Lord require of you? To act justly and to love mercy and to walk humbly with your God'. If you are a doer and not just a hearer of the Word of God, then you have to take poverty seriously.

God's love inspires it

God has commanded us to serve poor people and encourages us to share his heart for them. God has a special love for poor people, refugees, widows and orphans. Throughout the Bible, God responds to the cry of the oppressed. Will you love poor and oppressed people as he does?

It is hard for us to imagine God's feelings as he looks

down on the world. The Bible speaks of his satisfaction in creation; his anger in the face of sin; his joy in his people and his love for each person he has made. God sees all the injustice in the world, and the pain and suffering of every individual. Let's dare to ask him to allow us to share something of his heart for the world.

Sometimes we do feel something of the grief of God when we hear of the Rwanda genocide, the murder of street children in Latin America, or the impact of malnutrition in Ethiopia. Perhaps one incident brings it home, as it has for me when I have read of the torture and rape of a woman in Darfur, or the burning of a poor family's house by the army in Burma. But often we are unmoved, while God holds the suffering of the whole world in his heart all the time.

Jesus showed us the heart and character of God. His mission was to 'proclaim good news to the poor' (Luke 4:18). He wept over the reality of death at the tomb of Lazarus. He healed suffering people, restored their dignity and gave them the opportunity to earn a livelihood. He got angry with those who opposed such action because of religious tradition. He spoke to the socially excluded and outcasts, including lepers and the demon-possessed. Most of all he bore our sins on the cross so that we all, rich and poor, could be reconciled to God. Poverty reduction flows from the cross.

Change is possible

The third main motivation to act is that change is possible. Over the past thirty years, and despite the huge expansion in global population, we have seen incomes rise, educational standards improve, and death rates go down. The total number of people living in absolute poverty (less than a dollar a day) has fallen from 1.5 billion to 1.0 billion over the past 30 years, despite an increase in global population of 1.6 billion.[2.2] Economic management has improved markedly and democracy has replaced many dictatorships. Western governments are giving a higher priority to development, and many of them committed during 2005 to achieving the United Nations target of allocating 0.7 per cent of their national income to development assistance. Fairtrade is expanding rapidly amongst consumers in some countries.

Reductions in global poverty reflect millions of individual initiatives to supply clean drinking water in Uganda, establish sustainable businesses in Central Asia, provide treatment for tuberculosis through churches in Pakistan, and campaign for land rights in Honduras. Churches, including those that I have seen in Tanzania and Rwanda, have taken the initiative to serve poor people in their communities and see lives transformed. Churches in richer countries have hugely expanded their links with poorer countries, often through direct church-to-church links.

The huge expansion of financial services for poor people, including savings and small loans, has enabled many women to set up their own businesses. One of my memories of living in Bangladesh is sitting on mats with large groups of women as they engaged in training sessions and reported back on the progress of their investments in restaurants, animal rearing and other businesses. I saw not only an increase in their income but also a transformation of their social status, and many spoke of the greater respect which they enjoyed with their husbands and in the community.

The governments of the world have committed themselves to the Millennium Development Goals, with specific targets, including halving the proportion of people living in poverty by 2015. Although most of these global targets are likely to be missed, particularly in Sub-Saharan Africa, substantial progress is being made in reducing income poverty due to the rapid economic growth of China and, latterly, India. When the world's heads of state met at the Millennium Review Summit in 2005, they reaffirmed their commitment to these goals and pointed forward to the further progress required.

The challenges remain vast, with HIV infection continuing to rise, and over 100 million children still out of school, but history has shown that progress is possible when individuals and the world's governments prioritize the needs of poor people. Kerala in India has consistently achieved higher standards of health and education than other regions and countries on the same income level, while Pakistan has seen the reverse, because of a lack of investment in basic services for poor people.

The Millennium Development Goals (MDGs)

Heads of Government agreed the Millennium Development Goals at the United Nations Millennium summit in 2000. They consist of seven groups of global outcome-based targets. The first goal involves the halving of the proportion of people living in absolute poverty between 1990 and 2015. The other MDGs include targets for the reduction of infant and maternal deaths, limiting the spread of HIV, universal primary education, access to clean water and preservation of the environment. The final goal lays out responsibilities of richer nations to provide support and develop a framework of international law and other arrangements that foster poverty reduction. For more details, see the United Nations website at www.un.org/millenniumgoals/

Our technology and resources mean that we are the first generation in history where the substantial elimination of absolute poverty is a feasible goal. Our sinfulness means that, without God's grace, we are likely to miss the opportunity.

Personal integrity demands it

Our lives are not complete before God if we live in a world where others are suffering and dying of preventable causes, and we do nothing about it. We cannot just read about poverty.

We must do something about what we have heard if we are to preserve our own integrity. It's not easy, but we must change.

We often take our standards from those around us. You may be doing all right in comparison to other Christians. But what is God looking for in our generation when so many people, including Christians, are dying of hunger, when the environment is facing catastrophic change caused by our actions, when millions suffer from the impact of HIV and when hundreds of thousands of God's people face persecution? Rushing through hectic lives, in a culture obsessed by self-fulfilment and celebrity, it is easy to forget God's priorities for our lives. Let's stop, listen to his voice and discern what he expects of us.

This is also vital for the credibility of the church. I believe that God is calling his church, including you and me, to demonstrate lives of integrity in our generation. In Jeremiah 5, God challenges the prophet to go up and down the streets of Jerusalem to see 'if you can find one person who deals honestly and seeks the truth'. The implication is that he could not. What about today, in your city, in your church? If the church is to make an impact, it must offer an alternative way of life which has integrity in a world of inequality and suffering.

People who have made a difference

This book is aimed both at those wanting to change their everyday life, and at those willing to contemplate the extraordinary. It has been said that the people who make the biggest impact in life are 'monomaniacs with a mission'. Although most of us are not going to be like that, we can all make a difference.

There are countless examples to encourage us. I visited Jo and Lyn Lusi who are working with HEAL Africa in a hospital in Goma, in the eastern part of the Democratic Republic of Congo. They provide general medical services including HIV testing and care, reconstructive surgery and rehabilitation for victims of gender-based violence. They are training faith communities on HIV and gender issues, and I sat in one of their training sessions where a local Muslim leader was participating alongside church leaders. Their wider vision is to train doctors to re-staff the mission hospitals across the Democratic Republic of Congo. Jo is a doctor and former Congolese senator who played a part in drafting the nation's constitution; he read to us from a book of C.H. Spurgeon's sermons at breakfast time when I stayed in their home. He and Lyn saw their hospital buried in the volcanic eruption of 1994 and, although the patients got out by road, they themselves had to escape by boat onto the lake. The hospital is now rebuilt and they are providing a haven for those who have suffered in the current civil war, including those women who have been injured through sexual violence.

Edith Wakumire is the founder and Executive Director of the Uganda Women Concern Ministry. She was orphaned at the age of twelve but overcame her setbacks to obtain a degree in education from Makerere University in Uganda in 1979. From small beginnings in a family garage in Mbale in 1992, she has developed the Uganda Women Concern Ministry to empower orphaned girls and women and to help them acquire the information and skills that they need to improve their lives. The organization has grown to receive international recognition and a United Nations award in 1998 for reducing poverty amongst people living with HIV and AIDS in Uganda. Over 6,000 lives have been touched and many have undergone a process of spiritual transformation. In their own home, Edith and her husband have fostered seven children who were orphans, alongside their own biological children. They also housed nine refugees in their house for five years until they were resettled.

Tearfund has the privilege of working with such inspirational partners worldwide. Others include Michel Kayitaba who is working to bring reconciliation in Rwanda; Ieda Bochio who works in HIV prevention and training, and runs a home for HIV-positive children in Sao Paulo, Brazil; and Jeff

Woodke who has given his life to serve the Tuareg peoples in Niger as they battle to adapt their pastoralist lifestyle in the face of the encroaching Sahara Desert.

Then there are the ordinary people who are choosing to make a difference wherever they are through prayer, giving, lifestyle change and campaigning. They may never reach the headlines, but they are changing the world by their choices and service. Will you do the same?

Reducing Poverty as a Theme Throughout the Bible

The whole of the Bible speaks of God's passion to see poverty reduced. He wants the church and his people to take the lead in this area. Be encouraged that by engaging with these issues you are reflecting the heart of God. Justice and poverty reduction are themes that run throughout the Bible:

- The Old Testament Law provides the structure for a society in which private property and enterprise flourish, but within limits. The needs of people are always put above profit, whether in allowing gleaning in the fields or returning clothes taken in pledge. The idea of Jubilee, in which land would be returned to its original owners every fifty years (see Leviticus 25) has become an inspiration for the modern debt campaigns. It was designed to prevent the extremes of inequality that we see in this world and to ensure that everyone had a basic allocation of capital in the form of land that would allow them to make an income to live on. *'At the end of every seven years you must cancel debts' (Deuteronomy 15:1).*

- The books of Psalms and Proverbs speak of God's love and active concern for poor people and his desire that we should share this concern. *'The Lord secures justice for the poor and upholds the cause of the needy' (Psalm 140:12).*

- Micah and other prophets speak against inequality and injustice. Isaiah and Amos saw the rich getting richer and spoke out against exploitation of poor people and the dangers of luxury and conspicuous consumption. Isaiah 58 speaks of God's acceptable fast being to release the oppressed and to share your food with the hungry, sacrificing yourself for others: '...*if you spend yourselves on behalf of the hungry and satisfy the needs of the oppressed, then your light will rise in the darkness...' (Isaiah 58:10).*

- Jesus gave up the riches of heaven to become poor for us. He taught, healed and made friends with poor people. He called on us to love our neighbour and to give generously to brothers and sisters in the church. *'Whatever you did for one of the least of these...you did for me' (Matthew 25:40).*

- The book of Acts demonstrates that the early church practised concern for poor people through radical generosity and structured programmes: '...*there were no needy persons among them' (Acts 4:34).*

- The epistles exhort us to generous giving and speak about the early churches' system of giving. The church is to be a body demonstrating mutual love, solidarity and support. The gift for the Jerusalem church which Paul collected was driven by the needs of poor people in that church, and set in train a process of faith, provision and gratitude that provides a wonderful example of the blessings of generosity: '...*my God will meet all your needs according to the riches of his glory in Christ Jesus' (Philippians 4:19).*

- Revelation gives us a picture of a future world in which there will be no more poverty. *'There will be no more death or mourning or crying or pain...' (Revelation 21:4).*

CHAPTER 3

The Big Issues and How Christians Can Be Different

The most serious long-term problem facing the world is the desperate level of poverty and inequality, and the linked threat to the sustainability of the earth's environmental resources. Clare Short, *An Honourable Deception* (The Free Press, 2004, p. 257)

I worked for the Department for International Development throughout the time that Clare Short was the British Government's Development Minister from 1997 to 2003. She was a politician who used all her skills and abilities to create an independent development ministry in the UK focused on poverty reduction. She cared passionately about eliminating poverty and about using public resources effectively to do so.

She was exhilarating and sometimes a little bit scary to work for, and staff rightly feared her wrath. I remember once bringing a proposal to her for discussion, suggesting that the UK should provide additional aid to a poor, but badly governed, country. She started the meeting by vehemently outlining why she totally disagreed with the approach, and then asked me if I wanted to defend it. I did, but, as you might imagine, unsuccessfully.

Clare Short saw how poverty was a driver of many of the other problems facing the world. She was able to see the possibilities for poverty reduction with fresh eyes and ideas. We all become perhaps too familiar with the facts of poverty; the 1 billion people who live on less than a dollar a day, and the 30,000 children who die needlessly every day.[3.1] So in this chapter I look at poverty from four different angles that challenge each of us more directly: inequality, HIV and AIDS, climate change and conflict. I also outline a distinctive Christian approach to address them.

Inequality

Our desire is not that others might be relieved while you are hard pressed, but that there might be equality.
2 Corinthians 8:13

What is it really like to live on our planet in this century? Your experience probably does not reflect the daily struggles of most people on the planet.

Do you earn more than £10,000 or $20,000 per year? In that case you earn more than fifty times as much as the average income in the least developed countries. In 2005 the average annual income per person in the world was about $7,000, but this varied from an average of $35,000 in the high-income countries, to less than $400 in the least developed countries – a factor of almost 100. This hides even greater extremes: Luxembourg's figure was $65,630, while Ethiopia's was $160.[3.2]

Does inequality matter? For many years I felt that reducing absolute poverty was the priority, and that inequality did not matter. The Old Testament prophets suggest that it does. Amos and Isaiah prophesy God's judgment against the rich who indulge themselves while poor people are oppressed. It is clear from the Old Testament that God opposes absolute poverty, but also warns against excessive riches. There is inevitably going to be inequality in any society, but how much is reasonable? Are you happy earning five times more than a poor person, or twenty, or fifty? Some of us earn a hundred times more than our equivalents in much of Africa, and my daughter's monthly allowance at age sixteen (£60 per month) was more than the wages of half the workers on the planet.

Comparisons between South Korea and Zambia

The past thirty years have seen some dramatic shifts in world income and well-being. In 1975 the average income in South Korea was 3 times the average income in Zambia; by 2003 this ratio had risen to more than 20 times. During the same period, life expectancy rose from 63 to 77 in Korea and fell from 50 to 37 in Zambia.

There are many reasons for both countries' performance. Korea benefited from US support, land reform following the Korean war, and a strong focus on industrial competitiveness and international trade. Zambia experienced poor economic policy, the decline of the copper industry and the impact of HIV and AIDS. But the fact that economies can both grow and decline in such rapid and dramatic fashion shows the importance of good policies and the potential for change.[3.3]

The rapid income growth of China and India means that by some measures global inequality is falling, but the reality for most of the poorest countries is that they are falling further behind. This is not just a question of income, but of access to information, technology, financial services and the other elements of a modern economy. A friend from South Sudan remarked with a smile that if the 'Millennium bug' really had wiped out the world's computers, as was feared on the eve of the year 2000, then South Sudan would have been largely unaffected, because almost nobody had a computer, and few even had electricity.

If you are poor, you are:

- more likely to die at a young age;
- more vulnerable in a disaster;
- less likely to have your children go to good schools; and
- much less likely to own a computer, take a flight or win an Olympic medal.

Inequality continues in death as in life. The families of victims of the 9/11 attacks in New York received more than $1 million each. Assistance following other recent disasters has ranged from $1,241 per person for the 2004 tsunami, to $310 per person for the 2005 South Asia earthquake and only $53 per person for the ongoing crisis in Somalia.[3.4]

A different vision for inequality

God wants to see change for rich as well as poor people. The biblical vision for the world is not that everyone should live at European or North American standards. Proverbs 30:8–9 says: '...give me neither poverty nor riches, but give me only my daily bread. Otherwise, I may have too much and disown you and say "Who is the Lord?" Or I may become poor and steal, and so dishonour the name of my God.' That is a challenge both to remove absolute poverty and for Christians in the West to live more simply. We all need to change.

Friends from the Netherlands speak of how people there have very high levels of insurance to protect themselves against almost all eventualities. They feel that this lessens dependence on God, and can breed spiritual deadness. Wealth and security easily lead to hardness of heart towards those who are poorer than us. Christians have often modelled a different way by living more deeply in community, by sharing and giving. Whenever we do this on a large or small scale we demonstrate God's kingdom.

Just imagine for a moment that Christians took 2 Corinthians 8 seriously and decided to share their resources equally, even if only amongst all the Christians on earth. I have done some simple calculations, taking the statistics on numbers of Christians from *Operation World* (2001 edition) and the levels of income from the 2006 World Development Report.[3.5] Making the big assumption that Christians have the average income in the countries in which they live, then on average

Christians worldwide have an income of $11,500 compared with $6,400 for the world's population as a whole.

To make equality a reality among Christians, those of us in the UK would need to give away about two thirds of our income. But even if every Christian gave 10 per cent of his or her income to address poverty, then this would yield $2,300 billion per year, vastly outstripping government aid budgets which currently stand just above $100 billion.

How we respond to this inequality in the world will be one of the defining features of the church in this generation. It would only take evangelical Christians to give away 2 per cent of their income to poor people, to match the entire global official development assistance given by governments.

HIV and AIDS

The profile of HIV and AIDS in many Western countries is very low. But HIV, the virus which causes AIDS, is one of the biggest health crises facing the world, and one in which the church is part of the problem as well as being part of the solution. The church is contributing to unnecessary deaths through its teaching or lack of teaching in many countries about the sexual roles of men and women, and through restricting the use of condoms. Currently 40 million people are infected with HIV, with 5 million new infections and 4 million deaths from AIDS each year. The highest infection rates are in East and Southern Africa, but HIV continues to expand rapidly in Asia and Eastern Europe. In the West, those with the virus are kept alive with anti-retroviral drugs. In many developing countries, and despite a huge international effort to expand treatment, AIDS remains a death sentence for many. The church is a huge provider of care and support in the community for those living with HIV, or bereaved by AIDS. The World Bank has acknowledged the role of faith-based organizations, noting that 'their well developed on-the-ground networks make them uniquely positioned to influence values and behaviours and to mobilise communities'.[3.6]

AIDS is destroying key professions in many countries in Africa, killing large numbers of doctors, teachers and other vital workers. Life expectancies have fallen dramatically, back to levels that Europe last experienced 200 years ago. In Kenya life expectancy has fallen to 49, in Malawi 40, in Zimbabwe 38. Life expectancy in the UK is currently about 79. Of the 7 million people worldwide who need anti-retroviral drugs, only about 2 million have access to them, and less than 5 per cent of all mothers across West Africa are receiving the drugs that would prevent mother-to-child transmission of HIV.[3.7] In July 2005, the leaders of the eight most powerful industrialized countries committed to providing treatment for all by 2010. So far we are falling short. A primary target for our lobbying of governments should be to hold them to account to fulfil this promise.

The epidemic continues to expand rapidly among women and children. It is deeply shocking that African women face the greatest risk of being infected by getting married. Often, the church has not spoken out against male promiscuity, and has opposed the use of condoms. It has tolerated stigma and discrimination. Church teaching must challenge the sexual behaviour of men and the powerlessness of women in sexual relationships. Changing the attitudes to women in many societies, and increasing their ability to control their own exposure to infection, are key factors in reducing the spread of the disease. The church in many countries needs to get back to biblical principles and change its teaching.

AIDS is straining the supportive relationships of families and communities to breaking point. There are 12 million AIDS orphans (defined as having lost at least one parent to the disease) in Africa.[3.8] The number of child-headed households is rising rapidly. Grandparents have to resume work and parental responsibilities for their grandchildren, when their own children would previously have supported them in old age. For those living in the West, the impact of AIDS within African villages is unimaginable and largely ignored. I lived in Malawi at the beginning of the 1980s before the epidemic struck. Returning more recently, I was saddened by how many of my friends were going to funerals, and how AIDS was reversing many of the gains of development over the previous decades.

In 2005/6 there was a food crisis in Southern Africa, focused on Malawi and Zimbabwe. It was AIDS-affected communities that were the most vulnerable, because many of their key people were sick, many of their breadwinners were dead, and many of their assets had been traded in to pay for medical treatment. HIV and AIDS thrive where communities are already weakened by famine and conflict. In many conflicts, rape is being used as a weapon of terror and oppression, and HIV follows behind.

A different approach to HIV

HIV is the nearest modern-day equivalent to leprosy in the New Testament, in terms of its social impact. The church needs to start by being honest about the extent of HIV within the church, and the stigma that we often show to those who are HIV positive. HIV is a virus and not a sin. The church can take a lead, through both word and deed, in tackling the virus and giving support to some of the most vulnerable communities and individuals in the world. The church has a responsibility to bring hope to those living with HIV. We need to affirm that people can live positively with the disease, and to recognize the amazing efforts of those who are seeking to address its causes and reduce its spread.

There are some very encouraging stories to tell. ANERELA+ is a network of HIV-positive African religious leaders who are speaking out about the virus and challenging the church and the world. Churches are taking the lead in caring for the sick and adopting orphans. In Southern India, I met, through the Salvation Army, a woman who had thought about suicide when she discovered she was HIV positive. Now she and a group of other HIV-positive people are speaking out about the virus, and have taken responsibility for the care of fifty-one AIDS orphans.

In Burkina Faso, I joined a meeting in a church of about forty HIV-positive women and a handful of men, organized by Vigilance, a Tearfund partner. I heard stories of how they had been rejected from their communities, separated from their families and forced out of their jobs when their HIV status had been discovered. One woman spoke of having to sleep outside with her three-year-old child because her family had thrown her out. Another woman, weakened by HIV, had contracted tuberculosis. And yet in this church, people were finding friendship, acceptance and hope. There were opportunities to hear of God's love and also to explore the practicalities of seeking work, and even arranging marriages within this new community.

HIV challenges our attitudes, our actions and our churches, both globally and locally. There is an increasing prevalence rate in the UK, particularly within migrant and refugee communities. HIV provides a huge opportunity for churches to demonstrate extraordinary love and to bring their teaching in line with Christ's heart for the marginalized. You can help by praying, giving and campaigning for change in the church and in government, and, where possible, by caring for HIV-positive people in your own community. The epidemic is a wake-up call to the church to care more deeply for those who are suffering. We must respond.

Climate change

Climate change is a future threat to our planet, and a present reality for many of the poorest countries of the world. Communities are already suffering as a result of desertification in West Africa, greater irregularity of rains in Southern Africa and the impact of deforestation and soil erosion in Nepal. Poor people are finding that they cannot rely on traditional weather patterns. Climate change is not just about rising sea levels and the threat to low-lying countries, such as the Maldives. It is also about the spread of malaria as temperatures rise, the need to adjust crops to fit in with new weather patterns and the increasing severity of extreme weather events, which will primarily affect poor people. Climate change is as much a poverty issue as it is an environmental issue.

There are various causes of climate change, but human-induced emissions of greenhouse gases are both significant and growing. Some scientists argue that we are approaching the point of no return where global temperature increase will become self-reinforcing, leading to massive temperature rise that would make many of the tropical regions uninhabitable. Climate change is a controversial area, especially when we attempt to link it with the increasing frequency and intensity of natural disasters. But here are some facts:

- the global temperature is rising;
- this is at least in part due to increased concentrations of greenhouse gases caused by human action; and
- the rich Western nations are by far the biggest contributors to this (people in Europe contribute on average about ten times more per person to global warming than those in India).

The impact of climate change on poor communities is an interaction between their vulnerability and the severity of events. When rains fail, it is subsistence farmers on marginal land who face crop failures. When rivers flood, it is those who have been forced to live on the most vulnerable land who lose their livelihoods. If sea level rises, then Bangladesh could lose the 50 per cent of its rice production which is grown at less than 2 metres above sea level. Within Bangladesh, it will be the poor farmers, who have no options to relocate, who will suffer most.

Climate change will potentially lead to massive movements of people both within and between countries. Along with access to water, the movement of people due to changing weather patterns promises to be a major driver of conflict in future generations. In Burkina Faso I met a man who had lost all forty of his animals due to extended drought on the edge of the Sahara. Although benefiting from food aid to keep him alive, how was he to rebuild his capital and livelihood without a massive injection of external support? And how can traditional livelihoods be maintained in such semi-desert areas, given increasingly unpredictable rainfall?

A different vision for climate change

Climate change is linked to a growing incidence of severe weather events and other natural disasters. Disasters provide the church with numerous opportunities to serve. I saw a monument to the tsunami at Kanyakumari, at the southern tip of India, and I noticed that of the twenty-five agencies who had responded, thirteen were Christian. The church can demonstrate God's love through the compassionate response of giving, but also by getting involved in preparing communities for disasters and taking simple steps to reduce their vulnerability. This focus on 'Disaster Risk Reduction', which has been a priority for Tearfund, is becoming an increasing emphasis of the international community in the face of escalating disasters.

I am convinced that individuals and nations must reduce carbon emissions if the world is to limit the impact of increasing climate-related catastrophes. Christians can take a lead in this, by modelling the self-sacrifice that will be required to make changes. Rich countries are generally the polluters at present. People in India produce on average one tonne of carbon dioxide per person per year, while the Chinese produce four tonnes, Europeans ten tonnes and Americans twenty tonnes each.[3.9] If we are to move towards a stable global climate, then huge reductions beyond the existing Kyoto agreements will be required in the post-2012 period for those of us living in Western nations. This is going to be a long-term effort.

In Chapter 15, 'Living Sustainably', we will follow up the theme of climate change with an emphasis on individual action.

Conflict

There is a strong link between conflict and poverty. Between 1989 and 2003 there were over 100 active armed conflicts, the vast majority of which were in poor countries.[3.10] Conflict can seem distant in the West, but it is a daily reality for millions of people worldwide. Wars and violence destroy people and resources, discourage investment and disrupt economic activities. Since the collapse of Communism, ideological conflict has been replaced by civil war as the dominant form of conflict. Those countries that experience war are at a much higher risk of future wars. And conflicts in one country, such as Liberia, can often spill over into regional disputes, as troops, refugees and grievances move across borders.

Conflicts are often caused and prolonged by disputes over access to land or water. Even more pernicious is when control of diamonds, oil or other minerals both causes and sustains conflict, often involving forces from outside the country. The civil war in Angola in the 1990s was prolonged in part because of the resources generated from the exploitation of diamonds and oil, which gave many people strong economic incentives to continue the conflict.

Conflict opens the way to human rights abuses. People are more vulnerable, there is less media access and accountability, and justice systems have often broken down. It is vital that access is maintained for the Red Cross to operate in war zones and that there is not a blurring of the roles between soldiers and humanitarian agencies.

Sudan

Sudan has been embroiled in major internal conflict for the past twenty years, including civil war between the north and south and the more recent displacement of over 2 million people in Darfur. Sudan has been the scene of some of the worst human rights abuses of the new century, including the burning of villages and the systematic murder and rape of civilians. The presence of international agencies helps to limit the worst excesses of government and paramilitary forces, but there are acute dangers for aid workers. Tearfund has experienced the death of a staff member, but out of this tragedy also came reconciliation and forgiveness with affected communities as the team chose to return to those people who had initiated the violence.

Many of the roots of the Darfur conflict lie in the competition for land between nomadic animal herders, and settlers involved in cultivation. Tensions were manageable when there was enough land for all, but populations have risen and climatic changes have reduced the availability of land for agriculture, thus exacerbating the conflict. The central government has exploited these divisions, arming the Janjaweed militias, many of whom are drawn from landless tribes on the fringes of Darfur. Stories of suffering and oppression abound.

Even though there is currently a fragile peace in the South, the aftermath of conflict remains. When I visited one of Tearfund's sites in South Sudan, staff talked about recent incidents in which people with guns had accessed their compound and the fear that they felt. The previous year another site had been overrun and looted by militia, and there are regular incidents and rumours to which the communities and humanitarian teams have to respond. Pray for peace and justice in Sudan.

Conflicts leave behind a legacy of suffering. Once in circulation, guns are hard to remove. Demobilized troops often retain weapons and resort to criminal violence if there are no opportunities for work. Mines laid during the conflict lie hidden for years, waiting to maim and kill their victims.

A different vision for conflict

Conflict prevention and resolution depend on communication between communities, economic incentives for cooperation and, ideally, a commitment to forgiveness and love. The gospel provides the basis for such transformation. Christians have a unique tradition of conflict prevention and peace-building. South Africa has provided a Christian-led model of truth and reconciliation. At the core of the gospel is the breaking down of barriers between different groups of people inspired by the power of forgiveness.

Christians have developed the criteria for a 'just war' to limit the occasions on which states can establish a moral justification for conflict. Christians have often led the way in both preventing and resolving conflict from community level right up to international level. The high-profile abduction of the Christian peace activist, Norman Kember, in Iraq in November 2005 highlighted some of the key dilemmas about Christian peacemaking. What personal risks are justified in pursuit of peace and what obligations do states have to citizens who put their lives on the line in this way? But, most of all, his stand challenges us about whether we accept too easily the military interventions of our governments and about the price that we are willing to pay to promote peace.

Christians are called to bring hope into conflict. This can be through dialogue or the practical measures required to reintroduce economic incentives for peace. One of the greatest contributions to resolving the Kashmir dispute between India and Pakistan will come from those who encourage the cross-border trading that will give all the communities much greater incentives to maintain peace.

Canon Andrew White

Andrew White was the vicar of the local parish church when I lived in Clapham, South London. I then saw reports of his work in the Middle East when he moved to be Director of the International Centre for Reconciliation at Coventry Cathedral. He coordinates the Alexandria Process, which is a religious track that runs alongside the Middle East Peace Process. He has been vicar of St George's Church in Baghdad, a church characterized by both suffering and hope, and used to drive there wearing body armour and a helmet. In Iraq he experienced first hand the threats and persecution faced by Christians, and in 2007 he was forced to leave the country following death threats directed towards kidnap victims whose release he was seeking to negotiate. He has also been involved in mediation and conflict negotiations in Israel and Nigeria. He combines a commitment to interfaith dialogue and a passion for peace and justice, showing in a practical way how Christian ministry can be central to reconciliation and conflict resolution.

Conclusion

Despite the prosperity and peace of much of the West, the world is facing a range of complex and acute crises. These are affecting poor people most severely, reinforcing their vulnerability. These crises also provide opportunities for the church and Christians to demonstrate a different way of life, and provide almost limitless opportunities for service, giving, prayer and advocacy. Inequality gives us an opportunity to oppose consumerism and injustice; HIV challenges stigma within the church and allows us to serve the marginalized and rejected in society; climate change challenges our commitment to ever-increasing consumption and wealth; conflict prevention and resolution are vital for enabling poverty reduction and are a key area for Christian initiatives, often challenging the approaches of our own governments.

CHAPTER 4

What Causes Poverty and How Can It Be Reduced?

Currently more than eight million people around the world die each year because they are too poor to stay alive. Our generation can choose to end that extreme poverty by the year 2025.

Jeffrey Sachs, *The End of Poverty* (Penguin Books, 2005, p. 1)

Jeffrey Sachs is one of the world's most effective communicators on development issues. An economist and professor at Columbia University, he is passionate about poverty reduction. His book *The End of Poverty* came out of a massive research programme which he led for the United Nations to explore the feasibility of achieving the Millennium Development Goals, and going beyond them to see the end of poverty in our generation. He stresses the importance of 'clinical economics' – diagnosing the complex range of factors that make up a country's situation – rather than having a narrow economic agenda. He highlights in Africa the problems of isolation, poor infrastructure, disease, population growth and environmental degradation. His conclusions are that with good analysis, the spread of technology and enough resources, the institutional and physical constraints to development can be overcome, and poverty can be eliminated. And he translates that into practical programmes to make a difference, such as the distribution of antimalarial bed-nets.

Jeff Sachs has made a huge contribution to increasing the global focus on poverty reduction. He is a passionate speaker with access to the world's media. Much of his analysis is persuasive, and his objectives are good. For a Christian, however, I believe that there are two key ways in which his views are inadequate:

- He overemphasizes the importance of aid and assumes that if we spend enough money on a problem, it can be solved – that institutions can be created to overcome any problem. As such, he underestimates the impact of sin and the spiritual forces of evil, expressed through oppressive systems and structures, corruption and conflict.

- He doesn't give a clear sense of the objectives of development, beyond the immediate reduction of poverty. His goal is prosperity, but he has less to say about the need to challenge the negative dimensions of the consumerist lifestyles of the West, including environmental degradation. Is it desirable for everyone to have American living standards? Would that be possible or sustainable?

What is poverty?

Poverty has many dimensions. Economic poverty means lacking the income and assets necessary to sustain a basic quality of life. Poor people also suffer from food insecurity, poor health and education, inadequate housing and a lack of influence within society. They have limited economic opportunities and face social discrimination. They are vulnerable to disasters and economic shocks and are often powerless to change their own circumstances.

Within this group there are many people who are spiritually rich, in terms of their relationships with God and their communities. Similarly, there are many people who are economically affluent but who experience a poverty of relationships and in their experience of God. Sadly, there are many who are both spiritually and materially poor. A top priority of the church must be to bring whole-life transformation to these people.

Jeff Sachs is a potent symbol of the United Nations and the entire international development system. It has strong values and admirable objectives, but keeps coming up against the reality of human greed and oppression, and the selfishness of governments in both rich and poor countries, which limit its effectiveness.[4.1]

The objective of poverty reduction

The objective of development for the Christian is not to maximize people's standard of living measured in terms of consumption. Rather, the goal is for all people to live 'life... to the full' as promised by Jesus in John 10:10. This is centred on a restored relationship with God leading to a life of worship, generosity and service. It requires an economic standard of living that is high enough to meet basic needs and allows people to celebrate and share their resources with others. It also includes restored relationships in the community and a sustainable lifestyle that does not damage the environment.

God's plan for a transformed society is pictured in the laws of ancient Israel and the visions of the prophets. God's laws assume a market economy, but with limits on the accumulation of wealth and safeguards against destitution. When buying or selling, everyone needed to be concerned about the other person involved, and market forces were not allowed to depersonalize transactions.[4.2] For the individual it meant being born in a family where you received love and learned skills, an inheritance of land, and a network of community rights and obligations that gave meaning to life and provided security in old age.

This vision is spelt out as a future hope in Isaiah 65 where abundant life is pictured in terms of intimacy with God, long life, no more tears, an end to infant mortality, secure homes and livelihoods, and harmony with nature. This is a great pattern for poverty reduction now, and finds its fulfilment in the eternal vision of the new heavens and earth in Revelation 21 and 22, our true and final home.

What causes poverty?

The story of human poverty and prosperity is part of the wider story of humanity created by God, rebelling against him and having the hope of being restored through Jesus Christ. God has made us in his image with creativity that, when given the opportunity, has driven economic growth through enterprise and technological change. However, our sin and God's curse (see Genesis 3) have led to frustration, greed, inequality and oppression. The interaction of these two forces explains much of the pattern of poverty and wealth that we see today. Our societies and economic systems have been successful in creating great wealth, but are often characterized by the oppression of the poor by the rich. It is only through Jesus' work of redemption that we can find both spiritual and physical life in all its fullness.

Why are women farmers living in the villages of Tanzania generally poor? A look at the map and the distribution of poor countries suggests that some of the drivers of poverty are geographical and dependent on climate and natural resources. However, these are not decisive. Economic causes of poverty are exacerbated by social and political factors. Psalm 10 and Job 24 speak of the ways in which rich and arrogant people systematically oppress and exploit poor people, and call on God to intervene. Psalm 10:2 says, 'In their arrogance the wicked hunt down the weak'.

Societies often fail to address growing inequality, or to enforce legislation that recognizes the value of the individual and of the environment. Poor people face abuse of their rights by those with power. Family breakdown or bereavement can lead to the impoverishment of households, disproportionately affecting women. Discrimination by gender, caste, race or class denies people access to market opportunities. The Dalits in India are an example of a group within society whose poverty comes from systematic discrimination over many generations. Conflict and violence lead to suffering and destruction of assets, denying children the opportunity to go to school and disrupting community life.

Gender and poverty

An understanding of gender issues, and the roles of both men and women in society, is vital for poverty reduction. More women than men live in poverty. In many societies women are discriminated against in terms of education, food and involvement in politics. Jesus radically transformed the status of women and intends that we should do the same.

Gender perspectives in areas such as health, microfinance and patterns of work are essential if we are to address the root causes as well as the consequences of poverty. Projects designed to reduce poverty must take into account the different working patterns and responsibilities of men and women. Raising the status of women in society, particularly through female education, can have dramatic impacts in improving the health of communities as well as their economic progress. And specific action is required to address issues of reducing maternal mortality, eliminating female genital mutilation and encouraging male circumcision to reduce the transmission of HIV.

Poverty is passed on from generation to generation. The need for children to work, or the lack of money for school fees or uniforms, mean that they do not get the education that would allow them to raise their own productivity, health status and income. They are trapped in a cycle of poverty. Girl children are often denied schooling and forced into early marriage, limiting their life opportunities. Poor children grow up to be poor adults, who in turn have poor children.

Vulnerability and disasters

There are two dimensions to poverty. The first is described by someone's current situation, their income and assets. The second is about their vulnerability to future events. Large numbers of people are moving in and out of poverty at any one time. Many fall into poverty because of a specific crisis. This can be a fall in the price of the commodity that they produce, the illness or death of an income earner, the need to finance weddings or funerals, or the impact of a natural disaster.

Most people cope with such shocks through extended networks of family, friends and community who give support. In extreme cases, governments may provide relief and compensation. What else can be done? Established micro-finance schemes can provide loans in the face of disasters. Increasing the financial assets of poor people, so that they have 'money in the bank', can help enormously. A secure and accessible location for savings is often more important for poor people than access to loans. It is also encouraging to hear of innovative insurance schemes for crops being pioneered by groups such as Opportunity International (www.opportunity.org.uk).

The impact of natural disasters on poor people can be reduced. Such impact results from the interaction of the external threat and the vulnerability of the community. There is much that people can do to prepare for disasters and so reduce their vulnerability. This is known as Disaster Risk Reduction. Earthquakes in Japan are frequent and severe, but they do not generally lead to substantial loss of life because buildings are strong and people are well trained. I was shocked in Pakistan to see the way in which heavy roofs had collapsed on people during the Kashmir earthquake, because of inadequate building design, leading to substantial loss of life. Training contractors on how to build earthquake-proof houses, and training communities as to what action to take when disaster strikes, can save lives at low cost. Children in coastal regions need to be taught that when the sea pulls back and exposes a huge area of bare land, they should then flee inland and not go and look more closely, as many so tragically did in the 2004 tsunami.

Disasters are an opportunity as well as a crisis. For many communities they lead to strengthened mutual support and the start of a broader process of change. In richer countries people respond generously when they see the extreme suffering in poor communities and are then drawn in to a wider awareness and concern about poverty and development issues.

How can people be freed from poverty?

Rokeya sits breaking bricks by the side of the road in the sweltering heat of Bangladesh. Her children play amongst the rubble. Bangladesh consists of a massive river delta and has no stone. The broken bricks provide the basis for road building and a host of construction projects. For this woman and many like her, it is a job, paying the lowest of low wages. But how are Rokeya or her children to escape economic poverty? It is not by hard work. She is doing plenty of that. What she needs is for Bangladesh to develop so that it becomes an economy where the market is providing jobs at high wages, and has a political system that ensures that she gets the rights and opportunities that will allow her to benefit from such growth. There is a strong link between economic growth and the reduction of economic poverty. If Rokeya were living in a rich economy, she would be able to train for work that would pay her a reasonable wage, even if she started with a low level of skills.

Poverty reduction depends on:

- economic growth which avoids deepening inequality;

- effective government which ensures security, the rule of law and the provision of essential services to poor communities; and

- spiritual transformation of rich and poor people leading to individual dignity and the building of community.

Economic growth

Tearfund's feeding programme in Tieraliet, South Sudan

I stood next to Susan, the Tearfund nutritionist, as she explained the supplementary feeding programme for malnourished children in Tieraliet. Outside up to 300 brightly dressed mothers waited patiently for food in the heat with their babies. The team were weighing babies, one of whom sat docile in the plastic tub attached to scales, another of whom struggled to escape. Children lay down to be measured; mothers brought their blue cards for an update on their baby's height and weight, and to receive rations for the next two weeks. The team were doing a great job. They had been there for three years and seen some improvements, but that year things were getting worse again.

Susan explained that this was a chronic problem. As I looked at the long lines I wondered what it would take for this to be ended. Where do you start? With the poor standard of health and education services; with the lack of road access; with child marriage (girls marry from fourteen onwards); with low agricultural yields; or with the lack of clean water? The answer seems to be that you have to work on all of these, but that it is also essential to have people in the community who believe that change is possible and desirable.

Economic growth refers to the increase in incomes in a country over time. There is a strong link between economic growth and poverty reduction. No country has achieved sustained poverty reduction without growth. The impact of growth on poverty depends on whether inequality increases or not. Some countries have seen rapid economic growth that has primarily benefited those who are already well off, with limited benefits for poor people. In general, however, poor people also benefit as overall incomes rise. With higher incomes, people can afford healthcare and education to address some of the wider dimensions of poverty.

Economic growth depends on giving individuals and

companies the opportunity to take risks and invest. This works best in a market economy where people can trade both domestically and internationally. This in turn requires a basic system of laws and regulations that allow businesses to flourish. For poor people to increase their income, they need to increase both their skills and their access to capital. That means improving the quality of education for all, and providing access to credit through microfinance or conventional banking channels. International action is also needed to address injustices of trade and financial policies that discriminate against poor countries.

Economic growth will not meet the spiritual needs of communities, however, and is likely to become less effective even as a means of reducing economic poverty over time. In China economic growth has lifted perhaps four hundred million people out of absolute poverty over the last thirty years. Remaining poverty will increasingly be concentrated amongst the geographically and socially marginalised – remote communities, ethnic minorities, the disabled, children and the very old. This depth of poverty is much harder to solve through growth, and will require much more focussed interventions, including income transfers. It also requires community level action to provide support for vulnerable people. People who are not economically active deserve support because they are made in the image of God and have unique value. Income transfers to older people tend to benefit the community as a whole, because they are often spent in part on health and education for family members.

Effective government

Having an effective government matters for poor people. I was in Harare in 1981 on the first anniversary of Zimbabwe's independence. Despite a legacy of conflict, poverty and inequality, there was tremendous optimism. Zimbabwe had all the good points of Malawi, where I was living, and also had an industrial base, great natural beauty and tourism potential, and good newspapers. Now, as a result of Robert Mugabe's economic and social policies, it lies in ruins, with falling incomes, food shortages, and a third of the population living outside the country. Good governance requires leaders who are accountable to poor people, preferably through democratic systems in which citizens are well informed and empowered to take action at both local and national levels.

All people depend on governments for peace, security and access to justice and governments have a responsibility to maintain good policies and ensure the provision of essential social services that are accessible to the poor. Poor people need to be able to participate in the decisions that affect their lives at local and national level.

Different policy options in India and Malawi

Each country needs the freedom to pursue policies that are in its own best interests. India has illustrated the benefits of economic reform. At the beginning of the 1990s it had a huge, but largely uncompetitive, industrial sector. Economic reforms, including a greater openness to trade, have increased the efficiency of companies and provided incentives for them to increase exports. India's economy is booming, although widespread and severe poverty continues.

Malawi, however, is less likely to benefit from such policies. Its companies are small and weak and the most likely impact of rapid trade liberalization would be bankruptcies due to external competition. Although consumers would benefit in the short term, Malawi's longer-term development path may require some selective protection of infant industries. With rapid population growth, low agricultural output, little industrialization and high levels of HIV, Malawi continues to experience widespread and severe poverty.

There is a strong link between economic growth and good government. Private companies benefit from peace, good laws and an effective banking system. They can then create jobs and generate resources, through taxation, for health, education and other services. Governments can also restrain corruption, which can cripple economic growth, and support the courts so that people can get justice in the face of abuse.

Spiritual transformation

We have seen that poverty reduction depends on economic growth, and effective governments. But these alone will not solve poverty. There is a missing dimension. Poor people need increased incomes to live a more fulfilled life, but they also need love, acceptance, respect, friendship and a sense of belonging. These are the things that a purely economic model cannot provide, and which the pursuit of materialism can often take away.

Spiritual transformation is not the same as evangelism and conversion. We are all on a journey, and are transformed to different degrees. The question for each of us is 'Am I being transformed by God day by day?' Spiritual transformation is taking place when a husband stops beating his wife, when someone comes to know Jesus as their saviour, and when a Christian deepens his or her discipleship and learns to live more sacrificially.

There is a spiritual battle involved in poverty reduction. Spiritual forces, mediated through human greed and the pursuit of power, are at work to keep people poor, and lie behind many of the unequal structures of our societies. Corrupt governments and institutions have to be challenged and radically reformed. Brave people need to stand up against the powerful, supported by prayer. Communities must be built up through love and service. As poverty is reduced, the remaining poor will increasingly be the old, the disabled and the geographically remote. That means sacrificial love will be required to serve poor people in these communities.

We must be wary of simplistic links between the gospel,

economic growth and poverty reduction. Japan, with a very small Christian church, has flourished economically, while parts of Africa, with much higher Christian populations, have languished. So-called 'Christian' Presidents have often lacked competence and morality.

Some things in all societies need to change. I have never been more conscious of evil than when visiting a temple in Kathmandu in Nepal in the 1980s in which a young girl was kept enclosed and treated as a goddess until she reached puberty. But we tend to be more blind to the abuses in our own societies. The core of the gospel is good news for poor people everywhere. The church, when living as it should, can be a major agent for poverty reduction. The work of Bible translation has often been the opportunity for languages to be written down and preserved. It has provided the initial impetus for literacy and education in many countries, while also opening the way for the development of an indigenous church.

The gospel also helps to build community by breaking down the barriers between different ethnic and other groups. Some churches in Rwanda bear a terrible responsibility for complicity in the 1994 genocide. But now many are involved in reconciliation. At one church in the north of Rwanda, I saw two women embrace. One was Hutu, the other Tutsi, and one of them explained how as a child she had been taught to hate the other group. Seeds sown in children had come to fruition in the genocide, but now these two women had been brought together in Christ.

Integral mission

I have argued that sustained poverty reduction requires physical *and* spiritual transformation of individuals and communities. Theologians, particularly in Latin America, have called this 'integral mission', where the church both preaches and demonstrates the gospel to the world, and God brings spiritual and physical transformation.

The Micah declaration

The Micah Declaration on integral mission is a statement that was produced in September 2001 by the Micah Network, a coalition of churches and Christian agencies from around the world which work with poor people.[4.3] An extract is given below:

> It is not simply that evangelism and social involvement are to be done alongside each other. Rather, in integral mission our proclamation has social consequences as we call people to love and repentance in all areas of life. And our social involvement has evangelistic consequences as we bear witness to the transforming grace of Jesus Christ. If we ignore the world we betray the word of God which sends us out to serve the world. If we ignore the word of God we have nothing to bring to the world. Justice and justification by faith, worship and political action, the spiritual and the material, personal change and structural change belong together. As in the life of Jesus, being, doing and saying are at the heart of our integral task.

A vital dimension of integral mission is the work of the local church in contributing to the economic, physical, psychological, social and spiritual transformation of poor people. Integral mission is the prayerful and God-guided work of helping to restore broken relationships, and is a work that takes place at both a human and a cosmic level. The community of Jesus' disciples is the key context in which restored relationships are expressed, so the local church, as a caring, inclusive, servant-hearted and witnessing community, is central to the task of integral mission.

Integral mission gives us an action plan for reducing poverty through local churches based on preaching the gospel, building community, investing in people, challenging injustice and preparing for and responding to disasters. Our model is Jesus. Along with his compassion went action. Jesus met people where they were, asked questions, met their needs and spoke words of life. His manifesto was to bring good news to poor people, to heal the sick and to end poverty and oppression. He promised in John 14:12–14 that his followers would do even greater things.

Churches and Christian development agencies come in Christ's name and with his love. Organizations and individuals committed to integral mission will offer help to all on the basis of need regardless of gender, or ethnic or religious background. Integral mission means encouraging poor communities to develop their own assets and to look to be generous with what they have. It does not primarily look to outside support. Rich Christians are not the saviours of poor communities, but brothers and sisters who can walk alongside poor churches as we all seek to see God's kingdom come in our world.

CHAPTER 5

Who Needs to Do What?

The local church is the hope of the world.
Bill Hybels, Pastor of Willow Creek Church, Chicago

The Açao Evangelica (ACEV) is the best example that I have seen of a church denomination committed to poverty reduction. Its Portuguese name means literally 'action church'. Based in north-east Brazil, it goes into villages to plant churches and to meet the needs of the community, whatever they are. Very often, that has led ACEV to dig wells, but I went to one village, Immaculada, where they had built a children's playground. It was the only playground in the town, and there was a rota to ensure that every child had a chance to play with their friends. The exuberance of the children enjoying the excellent facilities provided by the church spoke powerfully of God's goodness. The church had also opened an after-school club and provided teaching support for local schoolchildren. Through this they had started to meet some of the parents, and the teachers told me of some of the family problems in the community and the way in which the church was able to provide support. This was a thriving church linked strongly to the community and meeting its needs – integral mission in action.

Traditional development theory has concentrated to varying degrees on the roles of governments, the private sector and civil society, including aid agencies, in reducing poverty. There is increasing recognition amongst development organizations, however, of the importance of the church and other faith-based organizations in poverty reduction. Churches act as a deliverer of services to poor people and a vital part of community infrastructure in many societies. The church can be much more than this, however. Tearfund's vision is to see 100,000 local churches in both rich and poor countries bringing physical and spiritual transformation to 50 million people in poverty over 10 years.

The PEACE plan

The PEACE plan has been developed by Rick Warren and Saddleback Church to see the church worldwide working to combat five 'giants': spiritual emptiness, self-centred leadership, poverty, disease and illiteracy. Their solution is to:

- Promote reconciliation
- Equip servant leaders
- Assist the poor
- Care for the sick
- Educate the next generation

Saddleback's vision is to see local churches and their members transformed from a passive role to one of active love and service in their communities. With an initial focus on Rwanda, Saddleback has sent thousands of volunteers to support churches in their efforts to deepen discipleship and to mobilize and serve their communities to see lasting change. The vision is to see 'ordinary people empowered by God making a difference wherever they are'. The challenge will be to ensure that this approach is sustainable and based on good development practice that achieves real change for poor people and the empowerment of churches and their communities. For more details of the PEACE Plan go to www.thepeaceplan.com.

Six key groups

There are six main groups involved in poverty reduction who have differing roles and responsibilities. It is important to see how they all fit together both to understand the process of poverty reduction and to locate your own role within it. These categories, which are all represented in both developed and developing countries, are:

- Private sector businesses
- Governments
- International development organizations such as the United Nations and the World Bank
- Civil society organizations
- Churches and other faith-based organizations
- Individuals

Although much writing on development focuses on aid (government-to-government development assistance), this is only a small part of the answer and can have negative side-effects. Real change happens when communities are mobilized, businesses invest and jobs are created.

1. Private sector businesses

Private businesses are the main driver of economic poverty reduction. Most private investment in any country will come from its own domestic sources. It is therefore vital to encourage local entrepreneurs if poverty is to be reduced. International companies can also have an important role. Recognition is often given to those providing charitable support to poor communities, but the business people who give poor people the opportunity to work their way out of poverty and create sustainable and productive employment have an even more important long-term role.

Businesses have responsibilities, governed by law, for their operations, their environmental impact and the conditions for their workers. Businesses can advise governments on good policies, but they also often lobby for narrow self-interest and seek to restrict competition. Businesses bribing politicians and public officials are the major source of corruption around the world. Companies have responsibilities to shareholders and society. Some businesses have ethical objectives, and may invest in additional facilities for their workers and families, and for the societies in which they operate. In line with the Old Testament principles, we should encourage businesses to be concerned for their workers and for poor people in society, and not to seek solely to maximize their profits. Businesses seeking to promote community development and support direct poverty reduction have a mixed record, and it is important that they employ development professionals to design these programmes.

What can multinational companies do right?

Western multinational companies are periodically blamed for paying low wages, repatriating excessive profits or having inadequate working conditions in poor countries. Responsible multinationals, however, can have a hugely positive impact. Providing basic commodities, such as soap, garments and food products, they can tap into the market created as people start to move out of the subsistence economy and into buying consumer goods. Their products improve the quality of life of customers. Employment and production boosts the local economy. With high ethical standards, they can help shape national employment and health and safety standards in the countries in which they work. Through training, they can impart management practices that will help employees to start their own companies in the future.

2. Governments

Governments of developing countries have the responsibility to provide essential public services, including health and education, and an enabling environment in which people enjoy freedom and are able to invest. We have seen how government's role is critical to poverty reduction in setting legal frameworks, limiting corruption, providing effective regulation and investing in water, sanitation, education and health. There is need for Christians to be engaged in politics and the civil service, and for others to support such people and hold them accountable.

Governments should prioritize the needs of poor people in their national budgets and planning. Many countries have developed a national poverty reduction strategy, which seeks to develop an integrated approach to addressing poverty. Such strategies involve the participation of many parts of society in their design. When effective, they provide a useful focus for poverty-reduction activities at the national level, and enable countries such as the UK to support the overall government budget with some confidence that this will produce positive impact for poor people.[5.1]

Governments in rich countries set the legal and financial rules of the international system. They have responsibilities, from trade negotiations to nuclear non-proliferation, to ensure that these meet the needs of the poorest countries as well as their own citizens. These governments are also the major donors to international development, both directly to poor countries and through the international institutions, which they generally tend to control. For more details of the UK government's aid policies and some excellent background information and policy work on poverty reduction, go to the website of the Department for International Development (www.dfid.gov.uk).

Development assistance is essential in disasters. It also has the potential in more normal times, where poor countries' governments are pursuing sensible policies, to speed the pace of change and reduce local the tax that needs to be raised to finance essential public services. With the resources from rich countries comes a range of policy advice and conditionality. The issues of the balance of power in such relationships and how the aid relationship affects the sovereignty of poorer countries are important ones in international relations. The benefits and limitations of aid are outlined in more detail in Annex 5.1, 'Does Aid Work?'.

3. The international system

Much of the world's development assistance and policy guidance is provided by the multilateral institutions which make up the international development system. This is one of humanity's greatest achievements and one of our largest frustrations. Largely created at the end of the Second World War, the international system consists of the United Nations and all its agencies, the World Bank and the International Monetary Fund, the Regional Development Banks and a number of other international organizations. Global public institutions are needed for peace and security (the United Nations), for regulation and standards (for example, in telecommunications), and for the provision of investment and development finance where market options are not available. They are primarily agents of national governments, but have huge capacity and resources to combat poverty and are funded by taxpayers from around the world. More recently the World Trade Organization has been created, which facilitates international trade negotiations.

Many of the ideals of the international system have been inspired by a Judeo-Christian view of justice and compassion. My own experience of the United Nations is that it incorporates the best of our dreams and the worst of our inefficiencies. The United Nations has a one-member, one-vote system and is often slow in acting due to diplomatic and bureaucratic wrangles. I have sat in huge international meetings with long speeches where delegates eat sandwiches or read newspapers. The United Nations is also very fragmented, with more than twenty separate agencies represented in some countries. On the other hand, the UN Security Council is the forum in which the greatest global crises are addressed and plays a vital role in standard-setting in areas such as health and migration. When crises strike, the UN has been effective in coordinating the international response and provides essential support to other agencies in the most vulnerable locations on earth.

The World Bank

The World Bank is a central part of the global development system, and has its headquarters across the road from the International Monetary Fund in Washington DC. Both institutions have been accused by development activists of forcing countries to undertake pro-market reforms, and not being responsive to the needs of poor countries. The World Bank is dominated by Western governments and has made many mistakes. Its mandate, however, is to eliminate global poverty, and it is perhaps the only institution in the world to have the resources, expertise and global reach to exercise leadership for the development community. It also plays a vital role in drawing together the knowledge and learning necessary to make development assistance more effective.

The World Bank has massive resources. In 2004/5 I represented the UK government in the negotiations to replenish the World Bank's resources. The UK government alone committed over £1.4 billion for three years (about £25 for every person in the UK). With this level of public money, it is vital that these institutions are accountable. The World Bank has a skilled and experienced workforce, but its policy is set by a Board in which the largest industrialized nations are dominant. A strong World Bank is essential to global poverty reduction, but it must reform its governance to give greater representation to poor countries. To find out more about the World Bank go to www.worldbank.org, and for a critical assessment of its work, look at the Bretton Woods Project website, www.brettonwoodsproject.org.

The international system is a mighty force for good in the world, but is subject to many problems including overlapping mandates and inefficient governance structures. It lacks the ability to hold corrupt dictators to account without the backing of major national governments. We must therefore campaign directly for multilateral institutions to act on behalf of poor people (for example, by writing to the President of the World Bank), but also indirectly through the national governments that sit on their boards (for example, by writing to your MP).

4. Civil society organizations

Wherever democracy flourishes, people create private organizations to achieve social ends. Civil society organizations (CSOs) include traditional charities such as Oxfam and Save the Children, but also community groups, research institutes, sports clubs and a host of other organizations. They are a great source of innovation, direct action and political pressure. They have often taken the lead in raising issues of crucial importance to poor communities including debt, climate change and clean water. CSOs in the South have a huge role to play in meeting the needs of poor people directly and holding governments to account. It is encouraging to see the continued rapid expansion of organizations such as BRAC in Bangladesh, who have pioneered financial services and non-formal education for poor communities and now have over 3 million clients.

The African Capacity Development Initiative

I first met Tokunboh Adeyemo, former General Secretary of the Association of Evangelicals in Africa, when he came to Malawi in 1981. He has identified the need for much more focus on leadership development and public ethics in Africa. As well as editing the highly recommended *African Bible Commentary*, he has founded the Centre for Biblical Transformation. This is a foundation working with African leaders from government, the private sector and civil society to support those wanting to change African societies from positions of influence. Bringing together leading African Christians from a range of countries and backgrounds, the initiative is confronting head-on the key issue of morals in African public life from a Christian perspective. Find out more at: www.cbtafrica.org

CSOs in rich countries also provide multiple functions. They raise resources for direct development work and act as a powerful force to raise development issues at the political and diplomatic level. Universities and research institutes, such as the Overseas Development Institute (www.odi.org.uk), play a leading role in analysing the causes of poverty and how they can be addressed. UK development agencies have taken a strong lead in major campaigns such as Make Poverty History. There is a key question of accountability for such CSOs, however, particularly when operating in developing countries, and it is vital that they seek to work as part of the broader national effort for poverty reduction. Many international CSOs, such as Tearfund, work in partnership with CSOs and churches in developing countries. These relationships allow for the flow of resources and capacity building, but also create opportunities for mutual accountability within partnerships.

5. Churches and other faith-based organizations

Faith-based organizations support people at the community level and during their times of most acute need. In addition to growth and public investment, poverty reduction requires:

- spiritual warfare through prayer;
- a willingness to stand up for justice and human rights; and
- a global network at community level to facilitate transformation and to care for the weakest.

The church can fulfil all these roles. With over 2 billion professing Christians in the world, there is no other organization with greater reach and commitment. The church can operate at global, national and local level. This requires responses from specialist Christian agencies, from denominations and church structures and, most of all, from local churches and Christians demonstrating practical love and care at the community level.

Churches in rich countries need to play a leading role to inspire Christians to get involved in campaigning, prayer and giving. Churches everywhere need to apply the word of God to today's global issues. They have unique opportunities to use their moral authority to call for change and to influence the political debate. At the local level they are often the agencies through which people become aware of development issues. They can form direct links across continents, as illustrated by the twinning of Anglican dioceses worldwide, creating a unique spiritual bond ahead of any development cooperation. They can pray for countries and communities in need and encourage members to get involved with development projects.

The local church and poverty reduction

Local churches can promote transformation that meets spiritual as well as physical needs. In many African countries, the church provides between 40 and 60 per cent of basic education and healthcare. The church is there for the key moments of life. Local churches are leading the way in HIV prevention and care work. Those suffering with AIDS will say that the church visits are appreciated because people pray with them as well as helping with health regimes. It is the local churches that bury those who die from AIDS, and provide prayer and pastoral support to the bereaved. Ordinary Christians are demonstrating extraordinary love as they adopt orphans and care for the sick and dying.

Local churches in Malawi, supported by Tearfund partner Eagles, are demonstrating how communities can grow more drought-resistant crops and introduce more effective water and sanitation systems. There are many villages in Africa where the church is the only local institution, committed to remaining in the community long after the international donors have gone.

6. Private individuals

Individuals and poor communities in developing countries will play a vital role in ending their own poverty. They can use their time and resources both directly and through their influence on government. For many Christians this may mean a willingness to serve in their own communities rather than seeking better-paid opportunities outside the country. But for many communities it is not their lack of effort that keeps them poor, and external support is also needed. Poor people's own efforts are a necessary, but not sufficient, part of any solution.

Where do the resources come from?

Joel Edwards, head of the UK Evangelical Alliance, spoke at the launch event for Tearfund's new vision in 2007. Reflecting on the feeding of the five thousand, he asked the question of where the resources had come from for this miracle. The loaves and the fishes came from a member of the community that was being fed. This is an important principle. Many churches in the poorest areas of the world, such as the slums of Delhi, are demonstrating a self-sufficiency that both maintains their dignity and provides a much more replicable model of church planting and growth than one that depends on external resources.

What do private individuals in the rich countries need to do? This is the subject of most of the rest of this book, but let me summarize by saying that we have a vital role in terms of our solidarity with poor people, our direct action and our influence on all the other institutions involved in development, particularly our own churches. We are called to pray, to give, to go and to campaign, as we will explore later on. As citizens in democracies we have the responsibility to influence the policies of our governments and the international institutions. Our responsibilities to developing countries' governments are more indirect, but we can seek to hold them to account for international commitments they have made and treaties they have signed up to. We can lobby big businesses and get involved with civil society organizations. We can also provide direct support to poor people and communities which complements these other efforts.

The Tearfund vision

Tearfund longs to see local churches fulfilling their God-given role to bring hope and change in the communities in which they live. We are passionate about the local church bringing justice and transforming lives – overcoming global poverty. This transformation includes the reduction of economic poverty, but also embraces restored relationships with God, within communities and with the environment.

Tearfund wants to see Christians and local churches throughout the world demonstrating radical discipleship by serving poor people. We want to see a global movement of people committed to living simply, joyfully and generously. We don't want rich Christians to feel that they have done their part if they have given to a development charity, but to be living a life of sacrificial discipleship in all its dimensions. This will include praying, serving, giving, campaigning and living sustainably.

Our ten-year vision is to see 50 million people released from material and spiritual poverty. To achieve this we want to see a global network of 100,000 local churches, in both rich and poor countries, proclaiming and demonstrating the gospel, and working together for change.

Tearfund is very conscious that we cannot do this alone. All around the world there are organizations of Christians who are seeking to meet the needs of poor people. Tearfund is privileged to be part of the Micah Network, which is a partnership of agencies from rich and poor countries committed to the local church and to poverty reduction through integral mission. There is a genuine sense of excitement as we all seek to serve Christ together, and look to see where he is taking this movement within his church and in the world.

What does this look like in practice? The gospel is powerful to change communities as well as individuals. In northern Rwanda, I met a Christian woman, inspired by the Scriptures, who had mobilized the women in her village to

build a water-supply system. The men of the village were challenged by this initiative, and committed themselves to building
houses for poor people. The community had then obeyed the
command to love their neighbour, and had taken their new-
found skills to serve a nearby village from a different tribe,
where they also provided housing and water supply. I saw how,
through this process, their church had become a place of
excitement and vibrant worship, and I was greeted by a chant-
ing group of perhaps 200 lining the road as we went to pray
together.

Tearfund has seen large numbers of churches in developing countries set on fire by biblical teaching about serving
poor people. When mobilized, some churches reach out and
serve others. Even more exciting, however, is where churches
start to mobilize the communities in which they live – where
Christians take responsibility within local government and
community organizations, being yeast in the whole loaf.

This vision to see 50 million people released from
poverty in the next ten years is a significant step towards the
elimination of extreme poverty. It is the vision that underpins
this book. I hope that in reading it you will want to join this
global movement too. Go to www.tearfund.org to find out
more.

Does Aid Work?

What is the effectiveness of aid in the form of external assistance to poor countries, whether from governments or international organizations?

Aid has been the subject of big swings in thinking and fashion. After the Second World War, the Marshall Plan, in which American funding helped to rebuild Europe's infrastructure, proved to be very successful. This led to a focus on investment to achieve industrialization and rapid growth in many countries. In the 1970s the pendulum swung the other way to emphasize the 'basic needs' of the poorest. In the 1980s came the rise of 'structural adjustment' with an emphasis on reducing the role of the state and getting incentives right for private-sector growth. This was criticized because of the negative impacts on poor people and the need to prioritize human development. From this evolved the so-called 'Washington consensus' which gave an important role to governments in supplying basic social services, such as health and education, and providing effective regulation for the private sector. Throughout these swings poor countries have suffered from the inconsistency of policy advice and the mixed motives and effectiveness of donors, especially during the Cold War.

Aid is not the most important factor in development. Peace is essential for sustainable economic growth, and many of the poorest countries of the world have been condemned to poverty by long-running conflicts. If there is a stable environment, then it is private investment based on the resources from within a society itself that will be key to its long-term growth. Alongside this will be opportunities for trade and foreign private investment. Aid will only ever be a minor part of the development story.

Does aid do more good than harm? One of the most cogent critics of aid was Peter Bauer, the distinguished right-wing economist.[5.1.1] He argued that aid is a transfer from poor people in rich countries to rich people in poor countries. Most aid is government-to-government, and encourages dependency and corruption. More seriously, it strengthens the role of government in developing-country societies and makes governments less accountable to their citizens. In this regard it can be similar to the discovery of natural resources (e.g. oil or diamonds) which give governments revenue without democratic accountability. Finally, it can lead to a rise of the real exchange rate that makes it harder for export industries to compete.

There is much truth in this analysis, but it fails to distinguish sufficiently between the case of governments which are committed to poverty reduction and those which are not. There is convincing evidence that aid works in good policy environments.[5.1.2] In the 1980s, donors imposed conditions on aid to try to ensure that it was well used. More recently it has been demonstrated that such conditionality is unlikely to work.[5.1.3] There is now increased emphasis on the importance of national design and ownership of poverty-reduction strategies.

The aid industry itself is also part of the problem. Much aid is given in a restricted way that benefits consultants and companies from the donor countries. The overheads and living standards of aid workers are often out of line with the people they are seeking to reach, and the aid community exists as a very privileged enclave within the poorest countries. Fleets of 4x4 cars and the rental of prime accommodation in the capital city by expatriate aid workers are familiar to all who have lived and travelled in developing countries.

How rich-country governments should provide support

to poor countries is also a matter of controversy. From an initial focus on individual projects which often conflicted with national development programmes, donor governments have moved in two main directions. The first group, including the UK, has provided direct budgetary support to developing countries. This reduces the requirement for poorer countries to raise taxation domestically to fund essential services, and therefore has an indirect benefit to the private sector. It has also supported domestic systems of audit and accountability which are essential for good governance in the longer term, rather than setting up independent systems which report only to the donors. Budgetary support, however, reduces the incentives to develop an effective tax system, runs the risk of making governments more accountable to outsiders than to their own people and makes it harder for donors to monitor the impact of their money. The second model, more favoured by the USA, is to support a wider range of actors within society, helping to promote directly the development of businesses and voluntary organizations as well as funding government work on a project or programme basis.

The very fact that aid exists is amazing. In an historical context, we can thank God that powerful nations are seeking to help others. We all know how hard it is to give things away without distorting relationships. This problem looms large in development. Aid works when it comes in support of a government or organization that is already committed to poverty reduction, but has inadequate resources. Aid is not effective as an incentive to persuade governments to change their behaviours. Aid runs the risk of strengthening the hand of government in society without making it more accountable to voters. To counteract these risks, there is a strong need to work through established relationships built on trust. This applies both at government-to-government level, and for NGOs providing assistance directly to community groups.

PART 2

Your Impact and Plans

CHAPTER 6

What Impact Are You Having?

We are all just ordinary people with the potential to do extraordinary things because we have an extraordinary God. Simon Guillebaud, *For What it's Worth*
(Monarch Books, 2006, pp. 13, 15)

If you want, or need, to be challenged by God, then go and listen to Simon Guillebaud. He is a passionate man committed to the gospel, and committed to poor people. All of my family have been stirred by hearing him speak at the New Wine festival in England. He lives in Burundi and his book tells the story of the work of God in the midst of poverty and war. I met him in Bujumbura when I visited Tearfund partners there in 2006. He challenged the expatriate Christians in Burundi about their commitment and lifestyle, and challenged me about the amount of money that I had spent on my hotel. He's right to say that we are not taking our discipleship seriously enough.

I strongly recommend his book, which is a passionate plea for more radical discipleship, backed up by real-life stories from Burundi and elsewhere. He tells of risks taken, of prayers answered and of the power of God at work in desperate situations. The book portrays the exhilaration and excitement of a life lived in total surrender to God, and challenges each of us to do likewise. Simon focuses on poverty in a chapter called 'A fair share'. He makes the link between liberal giving and the receipt of God's grace, asking why poor people are often more generous than rich people. He asks, 'How will future generations look back on a time when many in the West

are obsessed with avoiding obesity while much of the developing world doesn't have enough to eat?' (p. 162).

You and I only have one life for which we are responsible to God. What does it mean to commit our lives to the cause
of serving poor people? Given the opportunities that you have,
what impact are you having? Are you part of the problem, or
part of the solution with regard to global poverty? This chapter gives you the chance to reflect on your current impact and
priorities before launching into an action plan in the remain-
der of the book.

Your attitudes

*In your relationships with each other, have the same atti-
tude of mind Christ Jesus had.*   Philippians 2:5

Your attitudes will be critical to your impact in reducing
poverty. How do you feel about people who are much poorer
than you? Do you feel that poverty is their fault? Or that you
are superior? The gospel goes to the heart of the matter. We are
all dependent on God's grace, and any wealth and influence
that we have are gifts from him. 1 Corinthians 1 explains how
God chooses the weak and lowly to shame the strong and influential. How would you have fared if you had been born as a
peasant farmer in Mali? Even the lazy can be well off in a rich
society, while talented and hard-working people in developing
countries can remain extremely poor due to lack of opportunities.

Every generation and every society needs to recognize
its blind spots. One of ours is poverty. I believe that future generations will look back and be shocked that Christians were so
selfish. In a world where we could save lives and reduce suffering, we often choose not to do so, but to pamper ourselves.
It is time to weep and to be angry. God calls us to weep with
those who are suffering, and we need the Holy Spirit to ignite
the righteous anger that will drive us to action against

injustice. When was the last time that you wept or got angry on behalf of others?

Our attitude to HIV-positive or other marginalized people is a good test. HIV requires us to demonstrate solidarity with gay men, intravenous drug users and others who are suffering. How do you react to HIV-positive people, and what do you feel when poor and marginalized people come to your church? If they don't come, what keeps them away? HIV is a virus, not a sin. J.P. Heath, the General Secretary of ANERELA+, an organization for HIV-positive religious leaders in Africa, says that he will never answer the question, 'How did you get infected?' Why? Because people are asking it to find out whether he is innocent or guilty; whether he deserves their support, or whether they can judge him as one who is reaping the consequence of his own sinfulness. His comment cut me to my judgmental heart. How different I am from Jesus, who loved people where they were, and inspired them to change. God calls us to treat everyone as a human being worthy of our respect and support.

What is the current state of the West?

We are rich beyond the dreams of previous generations, with a high level of disposable income. We are materialistic, obsessed by celebrity. We are seeing the influence of the church on our culture reduce, and the influence of the prevailing culture on the church increase.

We face two principal dangers. The first is that we are distracted and absorbed in materialism that deadens us to the state of the world. The second is that we are secularized and lose our vibrant faith in a God who works miracles and intervenes powerfully on behalf of the weak. Some antidotes to these attitudes are to read the stories of those who are going against the tide, to stand with poor people, and to meditate on Jesus and his sacrifice in coming to earth.

Self-assessment

What impact are you having on global poverty? The ways in which you use your time, choose your relationships and spend your money will indicate your priorities and shape what you achieve. This chapter gives you the chance to reflect on these dimensions of your life and how they affect poor people. It may be that you already feel God challenging you about one of these elements, or it may be the first time that you have come across these ideas. Whether the questions are helpful or not, the key thing is to allow the Holy Spirit to encourage and challenge you.

Let's consider in more depth these three main dimensions of your life that you can use to serve poor people:

- your time and personal abilities;
- your relationships – the people you know and influence, and who influence you; and
- your financial assets – the money that you spend and save, including your impact on the environment.

These will then be broken down into nine areas that provide the basis for the action plan in Part 3 of the book.

Time and skills

Your time and abilities are your most valuable resource. God is seeking to give you the mind and priorities of Christ, which will include a heart for poor people. How are you doing in terms of using your time and skills for poor people? I suggest three measures that link into the action plan later in the book:

- Are you *praying* for justice, poverty reduction and change in poor countries?
- Are you *campaigning* on justice and poverty issues?
- Are you *serving* poor people directly, and willing to go wherever God asks you?

Rate yourself on each of these from 1 to 5 to assess the impact that you are having:

Current position	Not very active				Very active
	1	2	3	4	5
Praying					
Campaigning					
Serving					
Overall					

Working with others

The vision of this book is for a movement of Christians who are committed to loving God, each other and poor people. Significant things start to happen when we work together with others. It is through relationships that people and the world are changed. How are you doing in terms of working through your relationships to bring benefits for poor people? Here are three questions that link into the action plan later in the book:

- Are you *making friends* with poor people and those from other cultures, including refugees?
- Are you *encouraging other people*, including your family, friends and colleagues, to get involved in poverty issues?
- Are you *mobilizing your church* to serve poor people at home and overseas, and getting involved yourself?

Current position	Not very active				Very active
	1	2	3	4	5
Making friends					
Encouraging other people					
Mobilizing your church					
Overall					

Your use of money and your impact on the environment

The third dimension of your impact on poverty is how you use your money, and linked to this, the effect that you have on the environment. There is a strong biblical emphasis on living simply and being content. The Bible points us towards sustainable lifestyles which will maximize our positive impact on poorer countries and will not damage the environment. There needs to be a redistribution of resources from rich to poor as a response of justice as well as compassion. How are you doing in your use of money and your environmental impact? On a scale of 1 to 5, try answering the following questions linked to the action plan:

- Are you *living simply*, spending and investing strategically to maximize your positive impact on developing countries and your use of Fairtrade goods?
- Are you *living sustainably*, including seeking to minimize your carbon emissions?
- Are you *giving* generously for poverty reduction and human rights?

Current position	Not very active				Very active
	1	2	3	4	5
Living simply					
Living sustainably					
Giving					
Overall					

Becoming radical disciples

What do you conclude from your self-assessment? If you are like me, then the answer is that I am doing some things, and I could do much more. If poverty is to be reduced and the world changed, it will need your increased commitment. I want to challenge you to raise the priority that you give to the needs of poor people in your life, and to consciously cut out something else so that you can do so. Hebrews encourages us to 'throw off everything that hinders' (Hebrews 12:1). 2 Timothy 2:1–6 urges us to be disciplined in order to achieve what God has for us. God has been speaking to me for a long time about certain things that I need to cut out if I am to have space in my life for what is important. What takes up your spare moments? Will you make space in your diary to love and serve poor people by eliminating other things?

Our societies are obsessed with personal fulfilment, consumption and celebrity. Demonstrating a different way of life is perhaps the greatest gift that we can give to our society. We need to move our focus from:

- things to people;
- self to others;
- judgment to mercy; and
- consuming to sharing.

Repentance

We become Christians through repentance and faith. And it is through the same two instruments that the Holy Spirit leads us forward in discipleship to serve poor people. Being converted is only the beginning. God longs that his people should grow in their love and compassion. God calls his people to live differently and to show what his kingdom is like. He wants people to see his character through his church. Perhaps the greatest challenge facing the church in the West today is how to demonstrate radical discipleship in the midst of prosperity. How far will you go for God? Do you need a deeper repentance?

Take time to pray and commit yourself afresh to God for what he wants to do through you.

This is not just a personal matter. It is hard to work through these issues alone, and the ideal place to tackle the challenges in this book is in the context of a small group in your church. All Christians face the same struggles as we seek to deepen our discipleship. None of us are perfect, and we all need the encouragement and challenge of friends around us to make progress. The rest of the book should help to guide you into practical ways to put this into action individually, as a small group and in your church as a whole.

CHAPTER 7

Your Vision and Priorities

I know God will not give me anything I can't handle. I just wish that He didn't trust me so much. Mother Teresa

God in His glory will pour and pour His presence into people...that entire nations will be transformed.
Heidi and Rolland Baker, *There is always enough*
(Sovereign World, 2003, p. 177)

The amazing story of Heidi and Rolland Baker shows how God has responded to a couple who are utterly committed to him and to poor people, by doing great miracles. After a period of successful but gradual expansion in her work among orphans in Mozambique, Heidi had a dramatic experience of being filled with the Holy Spirit in Toronto in 1998. She was unable to move for seven days and says: 'This holy, fearful, awesome presence of God completely changed my life' (*There is always enough*, p. 68). She notes that until that time she and her husband had planted four churches in seventeen years. In the following five years they saw over 6,000 churches planted.

In March 2007 I went to hear Heidi Baker speak at the Elios Church in East London. She spoke about the adoption of children in Mozambique and our own adoption as God's children. What I had not been expecting was the sheer joy that she radiated. How could someone with such a massive ministry be enjoying herself so much? She pointed us back to God's goodness. It is not for us to deny ourselves, she said, so that in some way others will be blessed. God wants to bless us all with his presence, his love and his answers to prayers. Heidi's intimacy with God and the amazing things that he has done through her can be a real encouragement for us all.

In Tearfund we have wrestled with the story of the Bakers. How do you combine good planning with God's sovereignty? Do we wait for God's power to come or get on with the job? Heidi writes passionately of how God empowered her. Her ministry to poor people in Mozambique flows directly from God's work in her own life. But she also planned and prepared for future ministry through theological education and practical experience of serving God in other locations. Heidi prayed to go to Africa for twenty years before she started to work in Mozambique. Tearfund's conclusion was that God wants us to use all the expertise and planning tools we have, but also to humble ourselves before him. We need to wait and to acknowledge our dependence on him. Instead of our own agenda, we need to look for the places where he is working and get involved there, learning to give him the glory for what is achieved. For more about the Bakers and their work in Mozambique, go to www.irismin.org.

Seeking God

My friend and mentor Mike Wood was writing a book about Christian leadership at the same time as I was writing this one. It was a challenge to hear about the time that Mike spent in preparation with God before he wrote each chapter. Martin Luther sought to spend at least two hours in prayer every morning. The challenge for activists like me is to stop and wait to discern God's plan and receive his power. Or perhaps you feel that you can't cope, given the size of the task. God understands these feelings and wants you to press on in his strength. Your first response to the needs of the world must be a spiritual one – waiting on your knees before God. Why don't you take some time to seek God now? This part of the book is at least as important as all the action that follows. If you are an activist, then force yourself to stop. I mean it! If you find this hard to do on your own, then try talking and praying it through with a friend.

Developing a vision, priorities and an action plan

In order to plan in a way that will encourage, equip and inspire you as you go forward, I suggest the following four steps:

- Taking stock of your existing and prospective links.
- Asking God for a vision.
- Developing your priority and prayer list.
- Drafting your action plan.

All of these steps can be taken individually, with a friend or as part of a group. This journey is likely to be much more fun and encouraging in a group, since this will give you the chance to compare notes, learn from each other's ideas and do things together. You cannot change the world single-handedly, and you are not called to work alone.

Step 1: Taking stock of your existing and prospective links

You already have a unique range of contacts, interests and gifts that you can use in loving the world. The first step is to make a list of your existing links on a blank sheet of paper. Write down the countries with which you have special connections. List the friends that you have who are from different countries. Think of the people whom you support and pray for in other countries and add them to the list. Look at the organizations that you support financially or pray for, and write them down along with the key areas of work that they focus on. Then think about the activities that you are engaged in under each of these headings. You will probably be surprised by the wide range of connections that you already have.

What are you passionate about? What have you learnt from what you have done so far? What has worked well? What prayers have you seen answered? How have you seen God bless what you were doing? Jot down a list of things that you would like to get involved in, even if you feel you don't know where to start. Perhaps you could go back to the self-assessment sheets and think about the areas in which God may be calling you to step out further for him.

My existing links

Many of my links have been established during two spells living overseas. I lived in Malawi for two years after university and then in Bangladesh with my family for three years in the mid 1990s. We stay in contact with Christians in both countries, including the staff of our old church in Dhaka. I also love France and I have been trying to learn French for years. I am aware of some of the spiritual needs of France and other Francophone countries and I love to go on holiday in French-speaking areas. We have friends who are working in Central Asia. We live on the edge of the Somali community in South London and would like to get to know more about them and the nation of Somalia. I get regular information from Christian Solidarity Worldwide and Amnesty International, but I do not write to any prisoners. I am very interested in trade justice issues and the links with Fairtrade. I am also working at Tearfund and writing this book!

Step 2: Asking God for a vision

Ask God for a vision of the change that you long to see in the world. This process can take some time. Start with thinking about God's kingdom – where everyone has love and dignity. Think about some changes that you would love to see happen in the world to make it a better place. These may relate to the people, places, organizations or issues where you already have links, or they may be completely new. Dream big dreams. A vision is something that you long to see happening, that isn't happening at the moment. One of Tearfund's projects in Kenya on church and community mobilization has a specific focus on dreaming, with people sometimes lying down for a whole day to listen to God.

We all need a vision to guide us. Clarifying a vision is not easy, but is vital if we are to be motivated by the outcomes that we could achieve, rather than undertaking activities through a sense of duty and obligation. We tend to focus on the things that we can do, but it is much more inspiring to think about the changes that these can bring about.

Some ideas for vision might include:

- the physical and spiritual transformation of a specific people group, which might lead you towards supporting Bible translation, community development and poverty reduction work;
- the mobilization of your church to give consistent prayer and financial support to a people group overseas;
- the freeing of political prisoners and the introduction of democracy in a given country;
- the reduction in poverty in a specific village; or
- supporting a specific person or organization in their work to bring change and hope for poor communities.

Once you have some ideas, then share your vision with a friend or in your small group and start to pray that God will bring it into reality. If you find that you are short of ideas, then find a friend whose vision you can support.

Step 3: Developing your priority and prayer list

You can't do everything, but you can do something. By making choices and focusing on a limited number of countries, people and organizations, you have the chance to make a real differ-ence. After taking stock of your existing links and beginning to see your vision, then lay out your list of current and potential links before God. Pray about the various people, countries, organizations and themes, and let God show you what he wants you to concentrate on.

Focusing on development priorities

David Peck is the Archbishop of Canterbury's Development Secretary. He came to his job with a passion for the Great Lakes region in East Africa and has made this the primary focus of his work. He is clear that by concentrating on a lim-ited number of countries and issues, his team is likely to achieve much more. The East African region has a very strong Anglican church and a concentration of both natural and political challenges including conflict in Darfur, nation-building in South Sudan, regional droughts, fighting in the Democratic Republic of Congo, and reconstruction of the education system in Burundi. A full agenda; but David and his team have the opportunity to achieve real change because of the clear focus of their strategy.

The next step is to draft your list of priorities. My suggestion is that you organize items by the days of the week so that they can form a prayer guide. If you pray for up to two items a day, then that gives you a maximum of fourteen priorities within which to work, covering countries, organizations, people and issues, which seems about right. These will probably build on the relationships that you already have, but be open to God showing you new things, including countries and peoples that are less familiar to the English-speaking world. For each pri-ority you could also try to establish a top-level goal that you want to pray for. And be open to dropping and adding new pri-orities over time.

My work gives me lots of opportunities to connect with people and countries overseas. When I sat down to reflect on my priorities, I came up with the list below.

Peter's draft priority and prayer list		
	Prayer day	**Prayer targets**
Countries		
Bangladesh	Monday	Peace, democracy and t h e growth of the church.
Malawi	Tuesday	Overcoming poverty and HIV. Mobilization of the church.
Central Asia	Wednesday	Continuing freedom. Growth of the church. Employment and sustainable businesses.
Somalia	Thursday	Peace and justice. Education for poor communities.
Organizations		
Tearfund	Friday	For the Tearfund vision of seeing 100,000 local churches releasing 50 million people out of poverty to be fulfilled.
Christian Solidarity Worldwide	Saturday	Justice and freedom from fear for individuals and communities worldwide.
Operation Mobilisation	Sunday	Operation World and the work of OM worldwide.
People		
Abdul and Rebecca (Bangladesh)	Monday	Growth of the church and expansion of ministry to drug addicts and prisons.
Nelson Banda (Malawi)	Tuesday	Evangelism in Malawi and Mozambique.
Michael and Sarah Smith (Central Asia)	Wednesday	Bible school established.
Issues		
Trade justice	Thursday	A fair and generous world trading system.

HIV and AIDS	Friday	For the epidemic to be halted and those infected to have dignity and access to treatment.
Climate change	Saturday	Campaigning with Stop Climate Chaos. Global temperature rise to be limited to 2 degrees.
Francophone mission	Sunday	France, Algeria.
Vision: *What am I looking to see God do?*		
My vision is to see Christians and local churches forming a movement with truly global vision that lives sacrificially to serve poor people. Secondly, I want to see poverty ended and the church expanding and serving poor people in Bangladesh.		

I chose my areas and targets very widely. As you pray week by week, you can focus on smaller issues within these broad headings, or be prompted by specific issues that are in the news. You might find the table above to be a useful format to use for your priority and prayer list. A blank copy is at Annex 1 and it can easily be set up as a blank table on your computer. You can also download this template from: www.tearfund.org/poornomore.

Step 4: Drafting your action plan

With a vision and priorities, you have an opportunity in God's strength to change the world. What are the next steps? This is where the action plan comes in. This involves listing actions that you will take on a one-off, daily/weekly and monthly basis, with ideas for 'going deeper', across the nine categories in Part 3 of the book. It is the actions that you establish as habits that will make a difference in the long term.

The key to this approach is at the monthly level, and making a commitment to set aside at least two hours a month for a 'monthly action day'. You could try to do this on the last weekend of each month, or failing that, the first weekend of the next month. Some actions, such as praying or Fairtrade shopping, can be incorporated into your daily and weekly routines. Setting aside time once a month, however, gives you a chance to take some actions, such as campaigning and letter writing, which take more time, and also to review your progress and decide on further actions that you want to take.

I suggest that you do a first-draft action plan now, with the actions that you have done and are already doing. Then ask God to prompt you about what additionally he wants you to do as you read through the rest of the book. Jot down the ideas that really excite you, and then revise your plan when you reach the end of the book. Talk through your proposed actions with a friend and compare notes. You will benefit hugely from other people's ideas and encouragement. You can also work through these chapters in a group.

The template for the action plan is at Annex 2 and has boxes to fill in for actions that you intend to take. It can be set up easily in word processing software as a 13 by 5 table, or you can download it from: www.tearfund.org/poornomore.

My initial draft looked as follows:

Peter's action plan, draft 1:
Existing and previous actions

Sources of information	BBC website Operation World Magazines from organizations that I support			
Global action	One-off/ annual	Daily/weekly	Monthly action day	Going deeper
Praying		Weekly cycle of prayer for my priorities. Use of Tearfund prayer diary.		
Campaigning	Attendance at major rallies in central London			
Serving	Work-related visits to developing countries			Exploring local opportunities
Making friends	Inviting foreign students round for meals			
Encouraging others		Talking to my wife and children about global issues		
Mobilizing church				Speaking regularly about Tearfund at my church
Living simply	Moving my pension to an ethical fund	Buying Fairtrade bananas and coffee		
Living sustainably	Fitting energy-efficient light bulbs	Recycling		Changing energy supplier

Giving	Setting up standing orders and making a will			
Ideas for local action	Local homeless centre? Somali community?			
Other ideas to follow up	Savings jar Buying a bicycle			

I pray that as you work through the chapters you will see ways in which you can do some new things, and be encouraged, as I have been, as God takes you on a journey to help more people to be released from poverty.

PART 3

The Nine-Point Action Plan: What You Can Do

CHAPTER 8

Action 1: Praying

They can't eat prayer.   Tearfund, 1968

It's a big vision, so we are starting on our knees.
                                            Tearfund, 2007

Tearfund started in the late 1960s with a challenge to a complacent church that felt that praying, without action, was enough. When Tearfund launched its new vision in 2007, it was with a prayer initiative. A 'Global Poverty Prayer Chain' has been set up to encourage thousands of Christians around the world to pray together for people to be freed from poverty. For more details go to www.tearfund.org/praying. In the intervening years many churches had committed themselves to action on poverty, but, for some, prayer had been left behind. How can we become people who both pray and act?

What happens when we pray for peace and justice in Darfur or Zimbabwe, or for the release of a political prisoner in China? Firstly, it makes a difference in the world. God has chosen to act through our prayers, to give us a genuine role in his work. This may take time, but God has promised that he will hear and answer our prayers. Secondly, it changes us. We need God's love to care about poor people. We need God's power to be effective. These come through spending time with him.

How often do we pray to see poverty reduced and the lives of people changed? One of the best ways to pray for the world is to use the book *Operation World*,[8.1] which gives information and prayer targets for every nation on earth. Patrick

Johnstone, in his introduction to the 2001 edition, says, 'We do not engage in ministry and pray for God's blessing on it, prayer is the ministry from which all other ministries must flow.' Prayer opens the way for each of us to be part of God's plan. As *Operation World* says, 'When we pray, God works.' Don't let's get to the end of life and find that we pursued all our own good ideas but didn't do the one thing that would have made the biggest difference in eternity.

What the Bible teaches

1. We are responsible for praying

> *I urge...that...prayers...be made for...all those in author-
> ity, that we may live peaceful and quiet lives.*
> 1 Timothy 2:1–2

We are asked to pray for governments, even when they are not supporting poor people, for our enemies and for fellow Christians (James 5:16). The Bible encourages us to pray continually (1 Thessalonians 5:17) and persistently. We should not give up, even when God appears to be slow in answering our cries for justice (Luke 18:1–8). Jesus prayed regularly (Matthew 14:23).

2. God answers prayer and works miracles

> *If you believe, you will receive whatever you ask for in
> prayer.* Matthew 21:22

God has promised to answer prayer (Mark 11:24). We have many examples of answered prayer in the Bible to encourage us. Prayer will change us as well as the world (Acts 4:31). Prayer opens the way for new insights from God (2 Chronicles 20:13–14). Some things will only change through prayer (Mark 9:29).

3. Prayer is work

> *Epaphras...is always wrestling in prayer for you, that you*
> *may stand firm in all the will of God, mature and fully*
> *assured. I vouch for him that he is working hard for you.*
>
> Colossians 4:12–13

Prayer is the primary means that God has appointed to change the world. To pray is to exercise faith which pleases God (Hebrews 11:6). We need to be self-controlled to make time for prayer (1 Peter 4:7). God calls all of us to pray for fellow Christians and for the world (Ephesians 6:18).

The case for praying

Overcoming poverty is a battle. We face both spiritual forces and the deeply entrenched political and economic structures of our societies, some of which are shaped by human greed and selfishness. There are many situations where prayer is the most important action that we can take. For changes in government, or for the conduct of court cases, there is often nothing that we can do physically to influence the outcome. But we can pray. We are encouraged to pray for leaders, so let us pray for justice and effective governments worldwide.

All of us struggle to pray, and yet we know that our time with God is very significant. The amount we pray is a measure of our faith that God can change the world. If we have the habit of praying regularly, even for small periods, then this can make a huge difference. Prayer is the best investment that we can make of our time on earth.

We tend to pray about people and things that we care passionately about, and when we know that needs are urgent. If people are to be freed from poverty, then we must devote time to prayer. Prayer allows us to express our passion, our anger and sorrow about the needs of the world. It is uniquely powerful because it depends totally on faith. If God is not there, then it is a waste of time. Prayer is essential if our work is to survive eternally. All significant movements of God have been born out of prayer.

Answers to prayer at Viva

Viva brings together Christian organizations worldwide who are working with children at risk. Prayer is a central part of their strategy, including prayer chains and an annual 'World Weekend of Prayer for Children at Risk'. In the 2006 event, a group in Nyanza, Kenya prayed for blankets for flood-affected children, and moments later received a gift of forty blankets. Government policy was changed in Nigeria and India after specific prayer, and a pastor in Costa Rica was healed in response to the prayers of children in his church. For more details about Viva go to www.viva.org.

Actually praying and using your prayer list

In the previous chapter you have drawn up a list of your priorities in the form of a prayer guide. You can print this out and put it in your Bible to help you to pray for your countries, contacts and issues as part of your time with God. Prayer is hard work and requires persistence. To sustain your prayer, you need to believe that it is making a difference. So pray for specific things and keep a record of answers that you receive.

Your understanding of prayer depends critically on your vision of God and his relationship with you. Heidi Baker, who has had a tremendous impact working with orphans and church planting in Mozambique and beyond, says: 'My prayer is "help". God likes me and so He does.'[8.2] God likes you too, and cares about the vision that you have to see people and countries transformed. As you wrestle with him and work for change, he promises that he will answer your prayers.

Prayer is a journey in which we are all beginners. I believe your aim should be fourfold:

- to take the next step in praying more;
- to establish a habit of regular praying for the world, for poor and oppressed people, for the persecuted church and for those in prison, by using your prayer list;
- to start recording answers to prayer so that you can be encouraged and give glory to God; and
- to pray with others in some way.

Prayer encourages us to act. Increasingly, as we pray, we become God's partners in what he is doing here on earth. Sometimes, God will answer our prayers in ways we do not expect. Even when he does not answer directly, we can be confident that he is working for good in the situations we have prayed about. Often situations seem so hopeless that we do not know what to pray for. The Holy Spirit helps us in our weakness (Romans 8:26).

What should you pray for?

Pray for Christians in both rich and poor countries. Reading the New Testament, I am struck that Paul's prayers are usually focused on fellow Christians and their discipleship. The theme of this book is the role of the local church and individual Christians in poverty reduction, and so a key objective must be to pray for the quality of the church. Pray that rich Christians will have soft hearts when they hear of all that is happening in the world. Pray for Christians in the front line of the battle against global poverty. Working for Tearfund brings me into contact with numerous heroic men and women of God all around the world who are serving poor people, often in very difficult circumstances. Many church leaders in poor countries have to struggle against inertia and lack of resources. Temptations of higher-paid alternative jobs often beckon. Such leaders need your partnership in prayer, as you need theirs.

Pray for all people living in poverty. The facts are

perhaps too familiar: 1 billion people living on under a dollar a day; 30,000 children dying each day from causes directly related to poverty. How can you make those numbers real in your heart and in your prayers? A good exercise is to pray for people like you: to imagine people of the same sex, age and family position, but with no power, resources or education. Their desires are probably very similar to your own. For most, their opportunities are not. Think about some of the extreme events they face, and also the daily routine of struggling to earn a living while dealing with corrupt local officials and landlords. Imagine what it is like not to have money to buy essential medicine for your children. Turn those feelings into prayer for people in your priority countries.

Pray for elections and for leaders; pray for economic growth; pray for food security and good harvests; pray against corruption and conflict. Pray for God's kingdom to grow on earth; for his justice and his peace. Pray for the church to fulfil its God-given role; for godly Christian leaders in the church and in society. Pray for the political prisoners to whom you are writing; for the authorities of the countries to which you are committed. As your knowledge and prayer for a given situation both grow, you will not only be better informed but will also sense more of the heart and the will of God to guide your prayers.

Pray for peace. There is a strong link between conflict and poverty. As well as the direct effects of war, it inhibits investment and damages the economy. With conflict come human rights abuses. Christians have a special ministry as peacemakers, and peace is vital to achieving poverty reduction and human rights. Write down some of the major conflicts in the world as you read this and pray about them.

Zambia – a Christian nation?

Over 80 per cent of the population of Zambia are professing Christians. President Chiluba came to power in 1991 with a strong Christian manifesto, and declared the country to be a Christian nation. This was controversial even among church leaders within the country, and the global church looked on with dismay as President Chiluba's government slid into corruption and malpractice. What was our responsibility? Did we pray for him and his government? President Chiluba was forced to stand down at the end of his second term in 2001, and has faced extensive legal action alleging corruption and theft. Let us pray for Zambia now, that the current government will pursue righteousness and justice.

How to pray

So how do we move from a situation of not praying to one of praying? There are lots of possibilities, and for each of us, the route into prayer will be different. If you are good at research, then find out more about your countries and start to pray regularly on the basis of this information. Ask for a prayer guide from your chosen organization(s) and start to use it daily or weekly. Pick out the prayer points from magazines and add them to your prayer list. Have a specific slot to pray for poverty reduction and justice in your daily prayer time. Keep a prayer diary and ask for specific things. Keep in touch with the news to check for answers. *Operation World* provides the means of praying around the world, covering every country and various cross-cutting issues in a year.

What about letting the Bible inform your prayer time? Wait on God and ask him to guide you about what he wants you to pray for. As you read newspapers or watch TV, you can make these a gateway to prayer. You can voice an immediate prayer as a response to what you see, hear and think, as well as waiting for more formal prayer times. You can choose at least one article to pray for each time you read a newspaper.

Having set out your priorities and prayer list, you don't need much equipment to start. I suggest a Bible, an atlas and a copy of *Operation World*. Begin to collect information. Be open to adding other priorities as you go along, and see how God confirms your choices. It is exciting to see him connect you with relevant people and give you new opportunities as you pray and commit yourself to being his agent for change. Email is a fantastic facilitator for prayer. If you can get in contact with people on the front line, then you can pray in real time for their needs in a way that was impossible for previous generations. Many missionaries have set up restricted groups for people willing to pray for specific situations. Offer yourself to take part in such work.

Praying for Marie-Therese Nlandu

Marie-Therese Nlandu is a Congolese human rights lawyer and Christian who was a candidate in the 2006 Presidential elections in the Democratic Republic of Congo (DRC). After the victory of President Kabila, she was arrested, charged with treason and held in prison in Kinshasa. Marie-Therese, her husband and four children live in London, and a movement was set up by her church to pray for her release. At the peak of the campaign, the church's pastor received 700 e-mails in a single day. I went to the prayer meeting after she had been in prison for 100 days and experienced God guiding the meeting to pray for the nation and for the DRC President, that he might know God's heart of love. Through such prayer many people have come to know more about the DRC, and to hear about the life and witness of this extraordinary woman of God. On her release after five months in prison she spoke consistently for peaceful change and for the healing of Africa.

Encourage others to pray with you. It often takes real courage to suggest to others that we should pray, but it is worth it. And if you know of someone else who is using the same prayer guide as you, then keep in touch to compare notes. Get a country focus in your family or household prayer times, or at your

Christian Union at school or college. Encourage your church to pray. Offer to lead a prayer time and bring some materials with you to inspire others. Joining a prayer group can be great way to gain encouragement and encourage others. You can find details of local Tearfund prayer groups at www.tearfund.org/praying. Tell one other person that you plan to pray and ask them to pray with you on, say, a monthly basis. (Pray for some of their priorities as well as yours!) Learn from others, such as the 24-7 Prayer movement, about how to be more strategic in prayer. Above all, don't give up, and if you do, start again.

Being encouraged

We all need encouragements in prayer. It is great to read about those who have seen God move in some of the major historical events of the last hundred years:

- the Second World War, including the Dunkirk evacuation;
- the fall of the Berlin Wall, and collapse of communism throughout Eastern Europe;
- the end of apartheid in South Africa;
- the growth of the church in many nations under persecution, including China; and
- the opening up of countries previously closed to the gospel, such as Nepal.

Keep a record of prayers and answers received. Our prayers will be answered according to God's will and in his time. Celebrate when you see God's answers. Move forward gradually. In terms of your own commitment, don't promise the world and then fail, but try to make small changes and stick to them. There are urgent needs in many countries. Contemporary biographies, such as *The Heavenly Man* from China,[8.3] are a great encouragement for faith and prayer. The church is under massive persecution in many countries. Some will say that to rely on prayer is folly, but in the face of the forces of evil in the world, any approach other than relying on the God of the universe to intervene looks naïve and doomed to failure.

Recent years have seen a resurgence of the church's commitment to prayer. Organizations such as 24-7 Prayer have led the way in challenging young people to pray in new and radical ways with startling results. Tearfund now has about 180 prayer groups around the UK. The group in Inverness meets once a month and has provided prayer support to Tearfund workers in Afghanistan and Pakistan as well as praying for a range of issues and events. The group has also been a springboard for action in terms of volunteering and campaigning.

Pray at work. When at the Department for International Development, I was part of a small group that used to meet together every fortnight or so to pray for the organization and for the world. It is good to be able to pray for your own company and for the world. Can I suggest that you form a prayer group at work with this twin aim?

Examples where prayer has made a difference

The 2001 *Operation World* lists answers to prayer requests that appeared in the previous edition. In Malawi, it notes the courage of church leaders in the transition from dictatorship to democratic government. In South Africa, the establishment of genuine democracy post-apartheid and the progress in overcoming discrimination within churches. In India, the planting of more than 300,000 churches over the past 200 years and God's use of Christians to bring progress in health, education and social development. In Brazil, the way in which God has used intercessors to begin breaking the power of spiritism in Goias state.

Taking action

Prayer benefits hugely from new ideas. Organize an event for your church in which people have visual material to pray over. Create a prayer wall and stick prayer items and photographs on it. Link people to websites for up-to-date information, and feed back answers to prayer. Some of the ideas for action on prayer which you can include in your action plan are:

One-off actions

- Draft a prayer list.
- Start a personal prayer diary.
- Form or join a prayer group.

Daily/weekly

- Use a daily prayer diary from one of the organizations that you support.
- Pray round the world on a daily basis with *Operation World*.
- Pray through your priority and prayer list daily or weekly.
- Use a personal prayer diary.

Monthly

- Spend half an hour praying for the world.
- Have monthly focused prayer for your priorities.
- Meet with a friend to eat and pray.

Going deeper

- Go on prayer retreats.
- Get involved in 24-7 Prayer for your priorities.
- Get your church involved in a poverty prayer event.

- Read a book on prayer and do what it recommends.

Useful websites

- **www.24-7prayer.com**   24-7prayer.com is an essential website for prayer. It highlights those sites praying at any given time, and provides news, life stories and articles on prayer. Look out for the 'wailing wall' where you can post your prayers and join with those of others. This site also links to summary country information from *Operation World* for a wide range of countries.
- **www.gmi.org/ow**   The *Operation World* website provides links to the *Operation World* text for countries in the news and a daily prayer focus. For full text on all countries you need to get the CD or book, available through the website.
- **www.tearfund.org/praying**   Sign up for a weekly prayer email that features topical global items for prayer, to find a local prayer group in your area and to join the global poverty prayer chain.

CHAPTER 9

Action 2: Campaigning

You change a society by changing the wind.
Jim Wallis, *God's Politics* (Harper, 2005, p. 22)

Jim Wallis pictures politicians everywhere who are licking their fingers and holding them up to test which way the wind of public opinion is blowing. Effective campaigning is about changing the wind of public debate. Over the past ten years there has been a shift in the UK, inspired by public pressure, which has seen all the major political parties committing to giving the United Nations target of 0.7 per cent of national income as aid. This has partly been an outcome of the active campaigning of churches, NGOs and concerned individuals culminating in the Make Poverty History campaign and marches in 2005. We need to see this happen in all the other leading industrialized countries also.

Jim Wallis is an American pastor and civil rights campaigner who aims to build bridges between churches and politicians, and to span the divide between the US and Europe. I have heard him speak at Greenbelt, an annual Christian arts festival. He combines a warm humanity with a passion for poor and oppressed people. He loves God, but refuses to be typecast with one Christian faction or another. Why, he asks, cannot Christians care both about abortion and about the quality of life of people after they are born? He loves the Bible and he loves justice. In 2003 he came to the New Wine festival, which was much less familiar territory for him, and spoke passionately from the Old Testament prophets about the responsibility of the church to care for poor people. There are over 2,000 verses in the Bible on poverty and he argues convincingly that the Bible gives us no choice but to campaign on poverty and justice issues.

Jim Wallis wants to motivate the church as a whole. It is not enough just to have activists campaigning. Every church member needs to feel that a core part of their discipleship is to speak out and campaign on political issues that affect poor people. Christians should grow up seeing campaigning on poverty and justice as just as much a part of their discipleship as Bible reading and worship.

What the Bible teaches

1. God's heart is for justice

> *Let justice roll on like a river, righteousness like a never-failing stream!*   Amos 5:24

God wants to see justice for all. He intervenes on behalf of poor people. He gets angry when poor people are denied their rights and opportunities for access to him and to life in all its fullness (Isaiah 10:1–2). The prophets speak out against the oppression of poor people. (James 5:1–5).

2. There is a strong biblical mandate for campaigning

> *Speak up for those who cannot speak for themselves, for the rights of all who are destitute. Speak up and judge fairly; defend the rights of the poor and needy.*
> Proverbs 31:8–9

Proverbs tells you to speak out for those who have no voice. The prophetic tradition often involves bringing God's truth to those in powerful positions (1 Kings 18). Your aim should be to bring public policy in line with God's will, and to see governments applying just and righteous policies (Proverbs 29:4, 14).

3. We need to be doers and not just hearers of the word

Do not merely listen to the word ... Do what it says.

James 1:22

We are the salt of the earth, and the light of the world. We need to be courageous in the face of evil. We must care about justice for poor people (Proverbs 29:7). This gives us specific responsibilities for widows, orphans and refugees (Zechariah 7:10).

The case for campaigning

Governments have clear responsibilities towards poor people, and many of the wrongs of the world will only be righted through political action. The reluctance of many Christians in the West to be involved in politics is, thankfully, fading fast. The year 2000 marked the culmination of the highly successful, church-led Jubilee 2000 movement to reduce global debt. 2005 saw more Christians out on the streets than ever before to campaign on poverty and justice issues as part of the Make Poverty History campaign. 2007 marked the 200th anniversary of the abolition of the slave trade within the British Empire, which inspired a further church-led campaign to oppose modern-day people trafficking. Within a democracy we have a duty to stand for what is right. Any strategy for poverty reduction must include pressure groups, political lobbying and a passion for change.

We should not be afraid to cooperate with others outside the church while maintaining our distinctive identity. Working with others in a common cause is a great opportunity to make friends and to find our own prejudices challenged. From the parable of the good Samaritan, we can see not only that we should love others, but that Jesus was encouraging us to look at unlikely outsiders as examples of how to love. I once met a Canadian who grew up as a 'missionary kid' in a Christian school. He said that the one thing that his education had not prepared him for was meeting good non-Christians. We need to recognize that many non-Christians have been far ahead of the church on these issues. Let's work wholeheartedly with them, while bringing the additional dimension of the love of God into the campaign.

What should you be campaigning for?

Do you think that there are no big causes out there worth fighting for? Nothing could be further from the truth. Our society constantly puts the trivial centre stage, but God calls on us to speak out on issues of injustice that are affecting millions of people worldwide. Consider religious freedom, climate change, AIDS orphans, trade justice, finding a cure for malaria, children out of school, slavery and torture. Recent campaigns have highlighted the plight of the Acholi people in Northern Uganda, human rights in Burma, justice in Palestine, and the treatment of refugees in Europe. The list goes on.

Do not be intimidated by the increasing specialization and expertise required in professional fields. Ordinary individuals can make a huge difference as part of an organized effort and even on their own. Jody Williams was an American teacher and aid worker who cared passionately about landmines and whose action led to an international campaign, and eventually an inter-governmental treaty. Could you do more to campaign for justice, poverty reduction and human rights? It is good to support both church-based initiatives and to provide Christian support and inputs to broader high-profile campaigns. Why not join up today to Micah Challenge, I Count or the Trade Justice Movement? See their websites at the end of this chapter.

Lobbying your own government

Lobbying your own government is every citizen's duty, and a great privilege of democracy. Psalm 82 outlines the responsibilities of governments to defend the weak and the fatherless, the poor and the oppressed. In most countries a majority of people support greater priority being given to poverty reduction and human rights. But what actually happens will depend on the courage and competence of politicians and the pressure put upon them by us. There is no doubt that public pressure has pushed the UK Government to act on reducing poverty worldwide and given it the mandate to play a leading role in the international community on these issues.

In the UK we can start by writing to our Member of Parliament, the relevant minister or the Prime Minister on specific issues. This works best as part of a coordinated campaign. Very few people write letters. I heard it said when working for the UK Government, that one letter could be taken as indicative of 2,000 concerned people. You may well receive a standard reply from a civil servant in the relevant ministry, but these are often full of useful information for further prayer and campaigning. Government ministries keep records of the number of letters received on particular issues, so even a standard letter as part of a campaign will make a difference. Even better is for you to send a personalized letter that asks a very specific question or presses for some particular action, which then requires the Government to respond and allows you to follow up if necessary. If you write to your MP, ask them to forward your letter to the relevant minister, so you can increase its profile even further!

Politicians are also influenced by public demonstrations of concern. Joining with others to march or campaign is an exhilarating experience and one that can help to raise awareness and deepen your own knowledge of the issues.

Jubilee 2000

Jubilee 2000 was an outstanding campaign. Built on biblical principles, it drew great moral authority from the Old Testament examples of debt forgiveness and jubilee. It was founded by Christians, and the church played a leading role throughout. It then rapidly expanded to become a broad coalition that included trade unions, charities and many others. Starting in the UK, it spread through national campaigns in both rich and poor countries. By linking biblical principles to the plight of the poorest countries today, it highlighted an injustice which cried out for action. And it was effective. Debt cancellation to date has totalled tens of billions of dollars and funded free healthcare in Zambia, inoculations in Mozambique and education in Uganda, amongst many other examples.

Lobbying international organizations

International organizations are hugely important in developing countries. Institutions such as the World Bank provide large amounts of development finance for governments, increasingly as grants, but they also provide policy advice and help to shape development strategies. The large number of United Nations organizations provide specialist advice, and have a key role to play in conflict-affected countries and failing states. They can be lobbied directly by writing to the head of the organization concerned, or indirectly through your own government, which contributes to their budgets and probably has a role in their governance.

Campaigns have been mounted against the International Monetary Fund and the World Bank over the past thirty years because they have applied inflexible conditions to their lending to poor countries. They have sometimes required countries to cut spending on health and education, privatize companies and liberalize trade as part of a process known as 'structural adjustment'. The reality is complex. Such conditions have often been driven by economic crises. Difficult choices are needed and there is always an incentive for countries to blame the international institutions for unpopular decisions. But there is no doubt that World Bank and International Monetary Fund programmes have been designed with inadequate concern for poor people, and that spending on essential services has been cut while politically sensitive military and other expenditures have been maintained. Monitoring of public expenditure by community groups at the local level is vital if additional revenue, such as that from debt relief, is to be used effectively, and not spent on palaces, presidential jets or other low-priority items.

An important focus for campaigning is at the European level. A large proportion of European aid goes to the wealthier middle-income countries, and despite improvements and reform, there remains concern about the slow speed and responsiveness of European aid. On the other hand, Europe has taken a lead in the security aspects of development and has been generous in supporting debt relief. Why not write to your Member of the European Parliament (MEP) and the relevant European Commissioner to highlight the importance of development, and the need to put more resources into the poorest countries? You can find the name and contact details of your MEP at www.writetothem.com, which is a very useful website for contacting politicians who represent people based in the UK.

Can you campaign in developing countries?

The main people who can make a difference in any country are that country's own citizens. You can support individuals and organizations in developing countries as they work for change. Central to this will be links with churches in other countries. Many countries have branches of international organizations as well as local organizations which are campaigning for change. Search on the internet to see what you can find, and whether there are any indigenous Christian groups that you could pray for, or encourage through email and other means. Bear in mind that the content of emails may be scanned in many countries.

Information is vital to the fight against poverty and for human rights. Thank God for journalists who bring major world issues to our attention. Huge courage is required when the media challenge vested interests or enter conflict zones, and increasing numbers of journalists are being killed in the course of their work around the world. We need to recognize and support courageous journalism, and to draw on the information presented to us to create an agenda for change. How about campaigning on behalf of freedom of the press and the safety of journalists if you find them under threat in your focus countries? If you see a good programme on television, then write to the company to thank them and ask for more.

Human rights in Zimbabwe

While drafting an earlier chapter, I received a telephone call from our staff working with partners in Zimbabwe to tell me that a group of pastors had been arrested and held. Tearfund put out a press release deploring the government's action.

Pius Ncube, the Catholic Archbishop of Bulawayo, had spoken a little time before on UK national radio about the risk to his own life because of his outspoken stance against the government. He said that he was not afraid because he had the support of many people. But I asked him what would happen to someone less prominent. Harassment, cars outside your house, being watched, pressure and threats were the substance of his reply. How much easier not to stand up, or stand out. I was challenged. What does it mean for Christians in Zimbabwe to stand for God in our generation? To what extent are we not under pressure because we are not standing for justice and truth? And how much are we praying for situations like Zimbabwe and supporting our brothers and sisters there?

Foreign governments are often very sensitive to media coverage in the West. We can contact embassies, which often have very high-level channels back to their own governments. We can also write directly. It is good to write positive letters when tough decisions have been made, such as to prosecute those guilty of corruption. It is encouraging for a reforming government to get a letter of support and to know that you are praying for them. But there is also need to campaign for change when the reaction will not be so positive. It is good to take advice from those working closely with the country as to the most effective strategy for such letters, to combine them with prayer and to have clear objectives for your action.

Non-Governmental Organizations (NGOs) in Bangladesh

Bangladesh is in many ways the global capital of NGOs. Bangladeshis from the Grameen Bank onwards have pioneered innovative approaches to microfinance. This was recognized by the award of the Nobel Peace Prize to Mohammed Yunus, the founder of the Grameen Bank, in 2006. Such schemes involve savings and loans for very poor communities, often women. Groups are formed in which people guarantee each other's loans, making it possible for poor people to access credit and set up their own business. Organizations such as BRAC, a major Bangladeshi NGO, have millions of members and provide health and education alongside their financial services. But their success has depended on them taking a non-political stance towards government. It has been much harder for organizations that have spoken out against corruption and human rights abuses in a country that remains near the top of international surveys of corruption.

One of the most prominent country-based campaigns of the last forty years was that against apartheid. The protests around the South African embassy in London were a focus for the global campaign. Huge issues remain in Burma, Palestine, Sudan and many other countries which merit broader public support and require people who are willing to take a high profile in the international debate.

Religious persecution

Protecting human rights is a priority for campaigning in all countries. A concern for the suffering church worldwide may lead you to a particular focus on religious persecution. Despite the growth of democracy in the world, there remain high levels of persecution of religious minorities, particularly Christians. In the past generation we have seen rapid expansion of the church in Latin America, Africa and Asia. In each of these, and particularly in Asia, there has also been massive persecution of the church.

The World Evangelical Alliance estimates that over 200 million Christians in more than 60 countries are denied basic human rights as a result of their faith.[9.1] Persecution is strong in many Muslim-majority countries. There is also persecution, however, in communist states (including North Korea and China), in military dictatorships (Burma), and in Hindu (India), Buddhist (Sri Lanka) and other political and religious environments. The whole analogy of the church as a body implies that as one part hurts, we all hurt. We should be hurting a lot, given the current situation.

In Pakistan, religious minorities are threatened by blasphemy laws which are sometimes used to settle personal grievances. Once accused, individuals may face threats to themselves and their families. If imprisoned they can face violence and abuse. My experience of going to church in Pakistan included strict security and a consciousness of the vulnerability of the church to attack, alongside a determination of the church to worship God and be a witness to his grace. Converts to Christianity from Islam face ostracism or attack in many countries. Often individuals can feel as though there is no way through, without losing their home, family and livelihood.

Persecution in China

China's constitution guarantees religious freedom, but in practice the government continues to persecute the church. Treatment of churches varies from region to region. Government-controlled state churches are tolerated. Preaching by foreigners is banned. Unregistered house churches are subject to raids, harassment and arrests. There are numerous accounts of destruction of church buildings and torture of Christians. At the same time the church has known tremendous growth. Will we share the blessings and pain of our brothers and sisters in China?

Starting to campaign

The key thing is to do something. So few people are active that letters and campaigns can make a real difference. When you hear about situations, you may be moved but do nothing. How will anyone know about your concern? Many campaigns will take a long time and require determination and persistence. The record of the last ten years has shown how major campaigns can shift the political debate and lead to real impact on poor people.

Make Poverty History (2005)

The Make Poverty History campaign in the UK was part of the Global Call to Action on Poverty. Over 500 organizations were involved and for many thousands of people it was their first taste of campaigning on poverty issues. People around the world wore white wristbands. The Live 8 concerts and a huge march in Edinburgh focused attention on Africa as a preparation for the summit of the most powerful world leaders that was held in Scotland in July 2005. Worldwide pressure led to increased aid commitments by European governments, improved debt forgiveness and a commitment to providing AIDS treatment for all by 2010. Two years later, the movement followed up with a campaign called 'The World Can't Wait' to seek to hold governments to account for fulfilling these promises.

I suggest three initial actions. Micah Challenge is an international movement of Christians committed to seeing the Millennium Development Goals achieved. Go to www.micahchallenge.org.uk and sign the Micah Call to register your support for this campaign and be counted among the numbers of Christians worldwide who have signed up.

Secondly, why don't you write to your MP about the issue that is uppermost in your mind? As well as having an immediate impact, this will register you with him or her as someone who is interested in global issues. I occasionally get letters from my MP even when I haven't written, because he knows that I am interested.

The third immediate action is to sign up for a campaigning newsletter. Tearfund does a monthly e-newsletter called *Twelve* and has three different campaigning magazines. I recommend starting with *Global Action*, which comes quarterly and always includes an opportunity to respond. This could lead to regular campaign actions such as sending postcards, attending rallies and writing letters. You can sign up at www.tearfund.org/campaigning.

Taking action

I suggest that you aim to be involved in at least two or three campaigns at any one time. What to campaign on initially? Well, my priorities at present would be climate change, human rights in Zimbabwe and Burma, and securing peace and justice in Sudan. It would also be good to do some lobbying inside the church for Christians to do more on HIV and AIDS. But the choice is yours...

One-off actions

- Sign the Micah Call.
- Write to your Member of Parliament.

We are all connected. A British teenager looks out over an Indian slum. News, travel, trade and the internet mean that we can all be close to people in poor countries. Photo: Paul Brigham

Change is possible. I visited the market stall of this woman in north-eastern Brazil. She had been helped by a small loan from a church project and had created a highly successful vegetable business, generating an income for herself and her family. Photo: Peter Grant

It's people that make the difference. When I visited Brazil I met Ieda Bochio, who leads the Casa Filidelfia project in Sao Paulo. As well as providing a home for HIV positive children, the project provides training. These women had created an amazing array of bags, cushion covers and pillow cases which they were selling to generate income. I bought several – they made excellent presents. Photo: Peter Grant

The world is unequal, but how much inequality should we tolerate? It is not right that people should have to live in the squalor of slums such as this one in Mumbai, India, while others live in luxury. Photo: Tim Clarke

Boys playing in the flood waters in Mumbai, India where floods come regularly with the monsoon rains. These 2007 floods were associated with the displacement of more than 20 million people across India, Nepal and Bangladesh. Climate change is likely to mean more floods and droughts and a greater intensity of extreme weather events. Photo: Tim Clarke

Conflict affects many of the poorest countries in Africa. This smiling soldier provided an impromptu escort for a Tearfund colleague on a journey to the airstrip in Mundri, a conflict-affected region in south Sudan. Fighting had broken out between migratory groups looking for land where they could graze their cattle and establish a settled farming community. Photo: Fiona Perry

What causes poverty? Why are these Indian children as poor as their parents were? Greed, inequality, a lack of education, a lack of assets and access to credit, social discrimination and many other factors interact to reinforce the poverty trap. These are ultimately rooted in our broken relationships with God and each other. Photo: Paul Brigham

Poverty can be reduced through the use of simple technologies. This is a gourd which provides water for washing There is a hole at the bottom which is blocked with a twig when not in use. It only lets a small amount of water out at a time, making it perfect for hand washing. Any water that drops to the ground can be used to water plants, which as you can see, are growing well. This Sudanese boy is filling it up with water ready for use.
Photo: Fiona Perry

Education is vital for poverty reduction. This is a temporary school in an Afghan refugee camp just outside Quetta. Tearfund provided child-focused health education in the schools, which not only helped the health situation in the camps but also helped to improve the quality of the teaching given by the teachers. Photo: Fiona Perry

Private enterprise and agriculture are necessary for growth and a vital way of reducing poverty. These farmers, whom I met in Burkina Faso, are increasing their production and income by trying new crops and different methods of pest control. They are typical of millions of farmers and small enterprises around the world that provide people with the livelihoods they need to escape poverty. Photo: Peter Grant

Poverty reduction requires good government as well as economic development and spiritual transformation. Investment is needed in clean, reliable water supplies, and good government regulation is necessary to ensure that water reaches the poorest communities in an affordable way. This young boy, by the Nile in Sudan, is trying to pull his donkey out of the river bed with a heavy barrel of water, destined for sale in local villages. Photo: Peter Grant

A Tearfund prayer group in action in the UK. Praying in a group for poverty reduction and the needs of the world can make a difference and be a real encouragement to all who take part.
Photo: Geoff Crawford/Tearfund

Campaigning is about taking action, not just thinking about it. Writing postcards as part of a campaign can be a highly effective way of raising the public profile of an issue.   Photo: Tearfund

Make Poverty History brought more people onto the streets of Britain to campaign for poverty reduction than had ever been seen before. Churches and Christians were very prominent. This photograph is from the main march that was held in Edinburgh in advance of the World Leaders Summit in July 2005.
Photo: Tearfund

Right: A scene from the Stop Climate Chaos rally in Trafalgar Square in 2006 where churches and individual Christians were very prominent.   Photo: Peter Grant

Tearfund's campaign poster for the 200 rallies in advance of the G8 summit in Germany, using a strong biblical theme of justice drawn from the book of Amos and taking inspiration from the life of Martin Luther King.
Photo: Caroline Irby/Tearfund

There are many opportunities to serve in the UK. This project at St Rollox Church in Glasgow works with refugee communities providing practical support and skills training. They are developing deep relationships across different communities.
Photo: Tearfund

Transform trips provide an opportunity to participate in the work of churches and Christian development organisations in poor countries. Here, the summer 2006 team in Malawi get stuck into some practical work digging trenches
Photo: Margaret Passmore

This is one of a series of wall murals depicting the tsunami on the streets of Meulaboh in Indonesia. They show the horror of the disaster, but also include scenes of life getting back to normal as the community recovers.
Photo: Val Stevens

A project in Pakistan, led by Jane Jerrard, to improve the quality of primary education. I visited this enthusiastic class of children who were learning to read and write through a mixture of songs, rhymes and excellent picture-based materials. Photo: Peter Grant

A bus near my home in Streatham, South London, with the slogan, "We are the people we have been waiting for", first coined by Lisa Sullivan. In our globalised world, if you have a good idea, it can spread anywhere. Photo: Peter Grant

Encouraging children to have a vision for the world is a vital step to helping them get involved in global issues and poverty reduction later in life. Photo: Tearfund

A church in Pakistan meets to worship. Churches here face security threats and individuals can face persecution both in their families and through legal action under the country's laws against blasphemy.
Photo: Marcus Perkins/Tearfund

Children play in a playground built by a church in Immaculada, north-eastern Brazil. A rota was set up to ensure that all the children in the town had a chance to benefit from the facilities. It was great to see their enthusiasm and the way in which this initiative had helped the church to build links with the community. Photo: Peter Grant

Recycling: Brazilian style – a massive rubbish dump near Olinda. A thriving Anglican church has been planted in the community of people who work on the dump. Photo: Peter Grant

Recycling: British style – are you doing your bit? Photo: Tearfund

Members of my home church, Bedford Hill Baptist Church, demonstrate their support for Fairtrade.
Photo: Peter Grant

Ben Clowney was 'Fairtrade man'. During Fairtrade fortnight he survived by eating and drinking nothing but Fairtrade products and combined this by campaigning on trade issues.
Photo: Tearfund

This little boy is enthralled by the gift of pencils he has just received. He lives in a Tibetan community in the west of China where he goes to a school sponsored by the touring company, Intrepid Travel. They are committed to responsible and ethical travel and invest a share of their profits in the communities that they visit.
Photo: Val Stevens

Pastor Harry leads the Partners for Harvest Church in Fombe, Malawi. He has seen his community transformed by taking seriously the biblical responsibility to love our neighbour.
Photo: Marcus Perkins/Tearfund

Andrew is a farmer in Fombe, Malawi. He works hard to feed his wife, Grace and their daughter, Tadala. When floods dumped 12,000 tonnes of sand on his soil, his task was made much harder.
Photo: Marcus Perkins/Tearfund

I met Joyce Mbwilo at her home in Uhambingeto, in rural Tanzania. She featured in Tearfund's campaign for Make Poverty History in 2005. She used to walk fourteen miles a day to collect water, before a Tearfund-supported project installed a safe and reliable water supply in her village.
Photo: Caroline Irby/Tearfund

Christians in the UK, through Tearfund, support this project run by the Church of Pakistan. It was set up to treat TB and educate local men and women on a range of associated health issues.
Photo: Peter Grant

Financial support helps communities respond to disaster and prepare themselves for the future. While responding to the Kashmir earthquake, Tearfund sought feedback from the effected communities as to how their work could be improved. This suggestion box was one of the ways in which information was gathered.
Photo: Peter Grant

Dr Kiran Martin, the founder of Asha, with two women from the slums in Delhi. Over 200,000 slum dwellers have had their lives touched by Asha's work and there have been dramatic improvements in the health of women and children. Female volunteers from the communities have been empowered and have taken responsibility, both for themselves, and for the groups they serve.
Photo: Richard Hanson/Tearfund

- Sign up for a campaign newsletter.
- Adopt a country that you will campaign on.
- Buy a packet of blank postcards.
- Subscribe to a human rights magazine.

Daily/weekly

- Read a newspaper.
- Keep up to date on your campaign issues.

Monthly

- Have a regular letter- or postcard-writing slot to your MP and others.
- Take campaign actions for one or more campaigns.
- Advertise a campaign at church.
- Write a letter to campaign on a human rights issue.

Going deeper

- Get involved in marches and public demonstrations.
- Join a campaigning organization.
- Become a campaigns promoter with Tearfund.
- Organize a local campaign or join a local campaign group.

Useful websites

- **www.speak.org.uk**   Speak is a Christian campaigning and prayer organization that has focused on a range of poverty and development issues. It seeks to connect the emerging generation around global justice issues. Recent campaigns have included corporate accountability and lobbying the UK government to reduce its support for arms exports.

- **www.icount.org.uk**   I Count is the campaign of Stop Climate Chaos. It has a great website which gives information on climate change events and campaigns, provides practical tips for campaigning action and for changes in your own lifestyle and allows you to register on a map which shows the distribution of those who have signed up. I love their strap line: 'Find out how irresistible you are'.

- **www.tjm.org.uk**   The Trade Justice Movement is a UK organization that campaigns against unfair trade rules and to promote the accountability of private companies. It works on both global trade issues and the trading relationships between the European Union and poorer countries. Members include a wide range of UK organizations, including churches and major Christian development agencies.

- **www.barnabasfund.org**   Barnabas Fund serves the suffering church and makes their needs known to Christians around the world, encouraging them to pray. It provides practical help to strengthen and encourage the church in many different ways. Barnabas Fund was established in 1993 and channels aid to projects run by national Christians in more than forty countries. It has a particular focus on the Muslim world.

- Other human rights organizations include Christian Solidarity Worldwide (www.csw.org.uk), Release International (www.releaseinternational.org) and Jubilee Action (www.jubileecampaign.co.uk), which campaign on behalf of the persecuted church and persecuted Christians. Amnesty International is a worldwide movement of people who campaign for internationally recognized human rights (www.amnesty.org).

CHAPTER 10

Action 3: Serving

Jesus is not seeking distant acts of charity. He seeks concrete acts of love. Shane Claiborne, *The Irresistible Revolution* (Zondervan, 2006, p. 158)

There was a powerful silence as we sat in the Tearfund restaurant that Wednesday morning. Staff had gathered for our weekly prayers, and we were listening to a recording of Liz Jennings, who had gone on a Tearfund Transform trip, describing the scene around her at the end of her first week in Calcutta. The immediacy of her description of people living by the side of the road with no possessions, no access to water or sanitation and no security shocked us deeply.

She spoke of seeing two young boys, whom she had met, being tied up and severely beaten. What should she do? She had courage to enter the hut where the beating was taking place because she recalled the biblical promise that 'The Lord God is with you wherever you go.' She intervened and tried to stop the brutality. She discovered that they had been stealing money, and a passing policeman endorsed the punishment, which continued. And yet to Liz it seemed cruel and out of proportion to the crime. Liz wrestled with what would Jesus have done. What was right? How could she reconcile her values and standards with those she was facing here? There were no easy answers and probably none of us who were listening, many of whom had lived for long periods in developing countries, would have known what to do either.

Is it better not to know about these things, so that we

don't have to wrestle with impossible dilemmas? Surely not. We are called to follow Jesus; to serve and spend time with poor and excluded people, as he did; to see things as they really are and then to cry out to our God for change. We were so grateful to Liz, who had shown courage in going to India to serve those in need, and whose willingness to record her shock and confusion had allowed us to engage with that situation as well.

What the Bible teaches

1. Jesus commands us to serve

> *...serve one another humbly in love.* Galatians 5:13

Jesus said that we should not seek earthly power but serve each other in love. That is the true measure of greatness (Matthew 23:11). We need to be willing to go, not just to foreign countries, but wherever he sends us, including across the divides in our own communities (John 20:21).

2. We need to follow and imitate Jesus

> *You know the grace of our Lord Jesus Christ, that though he was rich, yet for your sake he became poor.*
> 2 Corinthians 8:9

Jesus came to serve and not to be served (Matthew 20:28). He spent his time with the excluded: tax collectors, prostitutes and lepers. We need to serve him and other people. Jesus chose to give up the glory of heaven, become poor and serve people, including us, who don't deserve it. As his followers we should demonstrate the same commitment to serving poor people, and must expect to share in his suffering and persecution as well as his reward (1 John 3:16,17; Philippians 2:5).

3. God will equip us to serve

The Spirit of the Lord is on me, because he has anointed me to proclaim good news to the poor.   Luke 4:18

God has given us his Spirit and gifts. There is a spiritual gift of serving (Romans 12:7). We have been given talents and will be judged according to how we have used them. Christian discipleship should be about trying to find God's will for our lives and then doing it. We need to go courageously and God will be with us (Hebrews 13:5).

Using your life and skills for God

Commitment to global poverty reduction does not necessarily mean living and working overseas. In many jobs there are ways in which you can bring in a global concern. For teachers that may mean adding development content to the curriculum and lesson plans. In multinational companies it may mean taking an interest in subsidiaries or partner companies in developing countries. For those working in the home or community it can mean raising issues with our friends or volunteering. For journalists it can mean an increased focus on development issues. In what ways could you bring poverty reduction issues into your daily work and activities?

We need to hear God's voice and practise radical obedience, whether that means to stay or to go anywhere in the world. We can all get involved in serving poor people in our own communities. Working overseas may require many years of preparation. If you are studying, then consider the options related to language and professional skills that would be of use in developing countries. Look at some of the adverts for jobs overseas to get an idea of the skills required. If God wants us to travel, live or work overseas, then he will provide the opportunities.

In my last year at university, Billy Graham led a mission

for the students. At the end of the week, he held a meeting for those who had been involved in the organization of the event. Instead of his usual altar call, he asked for everyone who was willing to serve God anywhere in the world to stand up. I did so, and the following day I heard that I would be going to Malawi for two years to work as an economist with the Malawi government. We don't always get such dramatic confirmation of God's call, but you can be sure that if you are asking him to guide you in these big choices, then he will.

Serving poor people in your own community

You must not ignore those in your own community who are poor. Soon after Matthew Frost took over as chief executive of Tearfund towards the end of 2005, he was asked: 'You say that you work with the poor – then what are their names?' Do you know the names of any poor people? What opportunities do you have to serve poor people in your own community, and are you taking them?

Tearfund has a group of twelve leaders from partner organizations around the world who come to our head office once a year to advise us on our work. Their first report in 2005 was startling. As well as focusing on our policies overseas, it asked very direct questions about what Tearfund was doing about poverty in the UK, about how British people look after their elderly relatives, and about Christian input into the UK education system. Tearfund has a UK and Ireland team, which has pioneered new ways of helping churches to serve their communities. It funds small projects focused on refugees and poor and marginalized communities in our inner cities, including dealing with debt, addiction and HIV. The team have seen significant impact though church mobilization in poor communities in the UK, which mirrors Tearfund's experience in poorer countries. But there is also a personal challenge to all of us about engagement with poor people in our own communities.

The opportunities are numerous. Elderly people are often lonely and require friendship. Refugee communities need support and advice. There are many examples of individuals and churches reaching out to poor people in their communities. I visited St Rollox Church in Glasgow where refugees, who are vulnerable to abuse in the community and deportation by the Government, get support, advice and skills training to help get them established in the UK. Goods are sold at low prices to the community for those who have limited income. It was great to watch a craft class and to see the strong friendships that have formed between women from numerous different nationalities, many of them not Christians, who have found a safe haven in the church.

One of the big challenges of working at Tearfund or any Christian development agency is personal integrity. How can we say we are serving poor people if we are not engaged in serving them in our own community? The risk is that we become tied up with global development, but it never gets to challenge us at the personal level. The conclusion that many at Tearfund have come to is that if we are serious about serving poor people, then it has to start where we are, in our own communities.

Serving where you are

I have a good friend called Paul, who faces physical disabilities and challenges that most of us would find difficult to overcome. As well as addressing these with patience and good humour, he has chosen to serve through volunteering for four days a week to work in a shop supporting Scope, a UK disability organization whose focus is people with cerebral palsy.

How can you get involved locally? Perhaps your church or a local community project has opportunities for you. If not, there are a range of Christian organizations which are active in our communities, including Christians Against Poverty, Grooms-Shaftesbury and Faithworks. The Besom Foundation provides opportunities to give time, money and possessions to support poorer communities. See details of their websites at the end of the chapter.

Visiting developing countries

Most of us have holidays. It is good to pray about how you use these, and whether God is calling you to visit a developing country. There are some important ethical and environmental issues to be addressed before you travel, but holidays are a key opportunity to go to new countries and to understand other cultures. You can visit and encourage friends, missionaries and church contacts. Many churches and organizations (including, for example, the Church Mission Society through its short-term mission schemes) provide opportunities to use our holidays and longer periods of time to visit churches and development projects around the world. Who knows what seeds God might plant through such a visit?

A few years ago I had a holiday visiting Central Asia to stay with friends. I saw a new church emerging from the ruins of communism with all the life and problems of the New Testament church. I saw the lack of employment and the need for sustainable businesses if these economies were to become prosperous in the new global market economy. My friends have been working to teach English and establish a Bible college; two key elements of a brighter future for the nation. My trip to this country, though brief, gave me a much greater understanding of the situation in the region, and many issues for prayer.

A further step would be to go on an extended visit, allowing you to see the church in action serving poor people, through the Tearfund Transform programme (www.tear-fund.org/transform) or equivalents from other organizations. These trips range from two weeks up to a year, and will take you to meet Christians in developing countries who are living by faith and serving God in poor communities, doing amazing things, often in extremely adverse conditions.

Going to a developing country for the first time can be a life-changing experience. It is much more fruitful if you can make contact with local people. When I first went to Malawi, I met a group of young Malawian Christians through a Scripture Union group in Lilongwe. I also joined a Presbyterian church for the first time and was amazed at how the traditions of Europe, including the pastor preaching in a university gown, had been transposed to Africa. Getting involved in a local church is a special privilege, as we suddenly experience the reality of our unity in Christ with people from a different culture whom we have never met before. Seeing the depth of love, suffering and spirituality of brothers and sisters around the world is a humbling experience, which helps to move the idea of partnership in the gospel from the head to the heart.

Visits by people from developing countries to our communities can also have a huge impact. Increasingly God seems to be calling evangelists from developing countries to replant the gospel in the West. Visitors to our churches can tell stories of God at work in regions of the world where there is a much greater level of faith and spiritual activity than in our own nations. In the early 1990s, a singing and dancing group from Uganda called Heartsong toured the UK. Through Altrincham Baptist Church, this led to a friendship link being established between Trafford Council in Greater Manchester and the town of Jinja in Uganda. Over 150 residents of Trafford have since visited Jinja, and there are growing links between schools, businesses and art groups. A charity, 'Act 4 Africa', was founded to work on AIDS prevention and is now active in most of East Africa. The visit also prompted a link between University College Hospital in London and Uganda. Three full-time missionaries have been called by God, and it was at one of their concerts that God spoke to Stella and me about going to Bangladesh.

Living and working in a developing country

Once you have visited, why not consider living and working in a developing country? As we seek God for guidance as to careers, we need to be open to the possibility that he might want us to work overseas.

Chris and Sonia Donnan

Chris and Sonia Donnan gave up their life in England to serve God with their three children in Kenya. Chris is very practical and got involved in teaching design and technology in an international school. Sonia has developed a new ministry with street children, called the Molo Street Children Project. The project has a drop-in centre which serves 20–30 children each day, and is working with families to help keep children off the street in the first place. Chris and Sonia are now considering how they can meet the needs of the large number of malnourished children that they meet. They are drawing on friendships and resources from the UK to support the work. I have no doubt that these connections through individuals and relationships are a key part of God's strategy. If you would like to know more about this work, go to www.molostreetchildren.org.uk.

God provides different opportunities during different parts of our life-cycles. These include school trips, gap years before or after university, university courses, volunteering, full-time service overseas, working abroad in professions and volunteering in retirement. For all of us, there will be periods when travelling and working abroad will not be possible. But for many there will be opportunities, some unexpected, that allow us to move overseas.

A good first step up is to give an extended period of time to volunteer. For young people volunteering can provide an excellent chance to sample development and get some initial experience on your CV. But there are also opportunities throughout life. With careers becoming more portable, and companies increasingly valuing diverse experience, then opportunities should increase. Volunteering organizations, such as Voluntary Service Overseas, no longer look primarily for young people, but for those with relevant skills and experience, including retired people who want to use some of their skills to help in development. Volunteering is now an option throughout your career.

Calling all lawyers

For those with some legal training, the Lawyers' Christian Fellowship offers opportunities to be part of a summer team or to work as an intern for a year in a Christian organization which is working to combat unfairness, corruption and mismanagement in East African legal systems. Further details can be found on their website at www.lawcf.org.

Many companies offer an international career path. This is a great way to get involved in a developing country, and to make friends, often in very senior positions in the countries in which you live. You will often have a privileged lifestyle, but you will also have resources and first-hand information on how to use them. By keeping links with your home church, you can encourage others and invite them out for a visit. When we lived in Bangladesh in the mid 1990s we were visited by a team from our church, which encouraged us and provided them with an experience that helped to spark a deeper commitment to mission.

Whether as a volunteer or in paid employment overseas, you will be able to make a difference wherever you are through your work. But you will also have the opportunity as a Christian to join a local church and share in the worship and ministry of another part of the body of Christ. Although a member of a Baptist church in the UK, I have been a Presbyterian in Malawi and a Pentecostal in Bangladesh, both being hugely enriching experiences. Christians Abroad is an organization whose main purpose is to give advice about both the opportunities to work abroad and the challenges that you will face (www.cabroad.co.uk).

Working in the development sector

Although any career may take you to a developing country, you can also choose to work directly in the development sector. I had the opportunity, as a young economist, of working for the Ministry of Trade, Industry and Tourism in Malawi for two years, through the Overseas Development Institute fellowship scheme. This is a professional scheme with some elements of volunteering, and is still running as an option for economists with a postgraduate degree.

If you want to work professionally in development, the options are broadly:

- volunteering;
- non-governmental organizations (NGOs);
- government: in the case of the UK, the Department for International Development (DFID), or as a diplomat with the Foreign and Commonwealth Office;
- the European Commission;
- international organizations;
- consultancies;
- teaching, including the teaching of English;
- research.

International organizations often have both young professional trainee schemes and mid-career opportunities. NGOs employ a lot of temporary staff. One of the major employers of development staff in the UK is the Department for International Development (DFID), the government ministry charged with development work. DFID recruits junior administrators but also a small number of junior managers through a Civil Service-wide competition. As well as direct entry to DFID, it is also possible to transfer from other parts of government from time to time. DFID also advertises (especially in *The Economist*) for a range of overseas posts.

Serving in South Sudan

Gladys is from the Turkana people of northern Kenya. She leads Tearfund's primary health work in Oriny in South Sudan. New primary health care units are being opened and workers trained to provide basic treatment to communities where preventable diseases such as malaria and diarrhoea still claim the lives of many people. This is a challenging environment; 40-degree heat, unreliable transportation links, conflict and security risks, scorpions, snakes and swarms of bees. I listened to Gladys as the sun went down and the team shared in their devotion time. She acknowledged the difficulties, but drew strength from the knowledge of God's calling to her to be in Oriny and the impact of the programmes. She reflected on her own sufferings in the context of Christ's sufferings for us, and expressed a calm determination to stay as long as God wanted her to be there.

I warmly recommend a career in development. There can be few better ways to spend your life than working for poverty reduction, and the intellectual and practical challenges involved are enough to stretch the most gifted and committed of people. You should not underestimate the frustrations, however. Aid agencies are often bureaucracies that vary in their effectiveness and cultural sensitivity. Corruption can distort worthwhile projects, and capacity in developing countries is often weak. Notwithstanding all these factors, the opportunity to engage with the great issues of our time and to work with inspiring partners from developing countries is a huge privilege and one for which I am very grateful.

For young people who want to go directly for development work, it is often hard to get that initial overseas experience. Look for internships or unpaid opportunities if your finances allow. Volunteer agencies provide such opportunities, but are looking for higher and higher skill levels over time.

Many people either volunteer for NGOs or go for jobs for which they are over-qualified. This can provide a sense of what it is like to work in development, but can also be hugely frustrating if the content of the work is not what you were looking for. So be realistic in your expectations of any job and be honest about your long-term career aspirations in discussion with any potential employer.

Showing what can be done

Jane Jerrard was a head teacher in Hertfordshire when God called her to use her life and skills to serve poor people. She arrived in Pakistan in January 1996, and since then she has been working for the Church of Pakistan's rural primary school programme in Sindh. Over this period, she has seen a system of training centres and village schools established to bring high-quality basic education to some of the poorest communities in the province.

I had the chance to visit her in Hyderabad in 2006. I saw motivated and enthusiastic children making great progress and obviously enjoying their school experience. Seeing the children's delight as they sang out the letters required to make a new word made me realize how much difference a teacher can make. Jane is excited to see the potential of these young lives being developed, and to share in Christ's mission to give hope to children and their families.

Reflecting on the way God has shaped her life and career, Jane commented: 'I realized that all my life up to the point of leaving England prepared me for my mission in Pakistan. He provided an open door and as I walked through it in obedience, I found it led to an abundant life. He gave me the opportunity to not only be a blessing, but to be blessed by many who have welcomed me into their hearts and homes. I have also experienced Christ's presence. He has provided for my physical, emotional and spiritual needs and enabled me to keep on learning and growing and thus fulfil his purpose for my life in ways I would never have imagined ... and the best is yet to come.'

It is useful to consider what professional and language skills you could develop that would be valuable in a developing-country context. This may lead you to get qualified first and then to look for opportunities in development. A degree in Development Studies may be less useful in the long term than a more specialist qualification that can then be applied in a development context. English teachers can help countries seeking to get more involved in the global economy. Investors bringing capital will be welcome in most countries. Professionals such as accountants, doctors and lawyers will similarly always be in demand, but may find it harder to work back at home again afterwards. This is a cost to be weighed up as part of planning your career.

Arts and the media

God uses the arts to awaken the conscience of a nation. They can play a vital role in reducing poverty. There are close links between worship, prophecy and poetry. Music, film, print and other media cut across boundaries in our globalized world, allowing the message of *Amazing Grace*, *The Lord of the Rings* and *The Passion of the Christ* to be heard by many millions. Foreign films and novels are a fascinating way in to the cultures which produce them. Do you know about Burkina Faso's film industry? If you want to understand the culture of an African country, then films and novels are a good entry point.

Within our own societies we can go to cultural events organized by different communities. Our local council in London used to organize weeks of Asian culture that allowed us to go and see a play by the Bengali poet Rabrindranath Tagore called *Tasha Desh*, and through that we were able to meet members of the Bengali community in our area. If you show an interest in the culture of any country, then you will be warmly welcomed. It is a great way to get a heart for a nation and to meet people.

Do you have creative talents that could highlight key poverty and human rights issues? Could you use your music, writing or painting to help others understand the issues? And how could you explore the work of others to deepen your own understanding? I have hugely appreciated the Greenbelt arts festival which has often been influential in opening my eyes to key global issues, including photo exhibitions in recent years on HIV and AIDS and the suffering of the Palestinian people.

One area for campaigning is to increase the coverage and depth of international affairs and culture in our own media. Some parts of the world get virtually no coverage in our media. British and French media present very different pictures of Africa based on historical and linguistic ties. Have you thought of writing a letter or an article for the press? Writing in English gives us access to a huge audience, and it could be the start of a writing career...

Taking action

The first task is to make yourself available to God and see what he does. If you have never been to a developing country, then I suggest that you aim to go in the next eighteen months. Book onto a Transform team or something similar, or plan your next holiday to give you an opportunity to visit a friend or missionary. Review your current commitments and see how well they match your priorities. This may lead on to looking for an opportunity to volunteer in your own community to serve poor people. In the longer term you may feel God's calling on your life to go abroad for an extended period or to commit to a community in your home country which will require language learning and some cross-cultural studies.

One-off actions

- Go on a mission trip.
- Review your use of time and make changes to your priorities.
- Contact a local organization involved in poverty issues.

Daily/weekly

- Share your work needs and pray for the work of others at your church.
- Pray for your community.

Monthly

- Undertake some regular service in the community.
- Visit a lonely person, or invite them over.
- Buy the *Big Issue* newspaper.

Going deeper

- Use your holidays for God.
- Learn a new language.
- Prepare for a career change.

Useful websites

- **www.vso.org**   Voluntary Service Overseas is the UK's leading volunteer agency. It is a development charity that works through volunteers with the goal of ending poverty. It is part of a federation which is working to globalize the volunteer approach and currently has 1,500 professionals working in 34 countries.

- **www.cabroad.co.uk** Christians Abroad is a specialist organization providing job adverts, advice and support services for those wishing to work overseas. It has a wide range of opportunities, particularly for volunteering, and access to insurance and other advice. A large proportion of the jobs advertised are in health and education.

- **www.besom.com** The Besom Foundation puts together those with resources with those with needs to 'sweep away suffering'. It gives opportunities for volunteering and for those who wish to give things, time or money to meet the needs of poor people. Initially based in London, it is now spreading around the UK. Besom have also produced a ten-week biblically based course – 'Simplicity, Love and Justice' – which has a primary focus on meeting needs in your local community.

- **www.capuk.org** Christians Against Poverty is a national debt counselling service with fifty-eight centres based in churches across the UK. They provide practical support to those facing debt issues, with a strong Christian ethos that emphasizes freedom from fear and personal empowerment.

- Other key websites for engaging in poverty issues in communities in the UK include Church Action on Poverty (www.church-poverty.org.uk), Faithworks (www.faithworks.info) and Grooms-Shaftesbury (www.grooms-shaftesbury.org.uk).

CHAPTER 11

Action 4: Making Friends

*God calls on us to be His partners to work for a new kind
of society where people count; where people matter more
than things...*
Desmond Tutu, *God Has a Dream* (Random House, 2004, p. 62)

I once had the privilege of sitting next to Desmond Tutu for a
day and a half at a conference in Nairobi. As he chatted infor-
mally he was gentle, kind and funny. As he intervened in the
debate he was razor sharp and passionate about injustice and
poverty. I think Jesus must have been like that. Desmond Tutu
gets angry and knows what to be angry about. At the same
time he took the trouble to write postcards to my two children
to thank them for their involvement in the Jubilee 2000 debt
campaign. They are treasured possessions.

Desmond Tutu believes in the transforming power of
love. He was able to bring Christian values to the centre of politics in South Africa and, in leading the Truth and
Reconciliation Commission, he has helped to create a model of
applied forgiveness which has been widely imitated.
Overcoming poverty means restoring relationships with God,
each other and the environment. Ultimately it's about people
and whether we care or not. God calls on us to put poor people first, to love people more than we love things, to commit
ourselves to freeing people from poverty in all its manifestations, and to plan our time and invest in relationships on this
basis.

What the Bible teaches

1. People matter to God

> *The Lord is good to all; he has compassion on all he has made.* Psalm 145:9

We are made in God's image and he loves each of us (Jude 1). Each person is of immense value to God. Relationships are at the heart of the gospel. He cares for the lost sheep and does not want to see anyone perish (Matthew 18:12–14). God loved the world so much that he sent Jesus to die for us (John 3:16).

2. We are called to serve poor people in love

> *If I give all I possess to the poor ... but do not have love, I gain nothing.* 1 Corinthians 13:3

God cares about relationships. The most important commandments are to love God and to love our neighbour (Mark 12:29–31). We are called to welcome strangers and practise hospitality (Romans 12:13; Hebrews 13:1–2). Without love for people, nothing else we do counts for anything. God calls on you to lay down your life for others in love. By serving poor people you are serving the Lord (Proverbs 19:17).

3. We are called to visit and care for prisoners

> *Remember those in prison as if you were together with them in prison, and those who are ill-treated as if you yourselves were suffering.* Hebrews 13:3

God encourages us to care for and visit prisoners and to remember them in our prayers. The New Testament expects persecution to be the normal experience of Christians (2 Timothy 3:12). Those not affected are called upon to pray and to stand with their brothers and sisters undergoing trials. The

Bible calls us to 'mourn with those who mourn' (Romans 12:15).

Making friends

Poverty reduction includes restoring relationships with God, and between people. Poverty reduction comes alive when we make friends with people. Either through travelling, or through welcoming visitors into your home, you can make friends with poor people and with those working directly in poor communities. So when I hear about Peru, I think of Alphonso Weiland who has set up an organization called Peace and Hope to campaign for human rights, especially those of indigenous peoples. When I hear of India, I know that Dino Touthang, and his organization Eficor, will be involved in crisis response and serving the poorest. Why don't you volunteer the next time your church is looking for someone to provide accommodation or meals for a visitor from abroad? You will be tremendously blessed, and email makes it easier than ever to maintain such relationships after an initial contact.

We often wonder what can make Christians distinctive in the world and allow people to see Christ. The answer is loving people, especially the unlovable. If poverty is rooted in broken relationships, then it is love expressed through practical works of service that will be the solution. By loving non-Christians we have the chance to break out from patterns of rivalry between religions, and by loving Christians we can build family, so that all people will know that we are his disciples.

A volunteer with the Evangelical Fellowship of Zambia decided to look after a man with HIV who had been abandoned by his family and community. Initially he was shocked by the stench of his clothes and sheets, but he washed him, fed him and spoke to him of a Saviour who loved him. The volunteer said: 'Daily I visited him. He died three weeks later, not an outcast, but one loved and created in God's image. When I told him God loved him and that Jesus died for him, he held my hand tight.'

We are called to have a special concern for Christians as our brothers and sisters: 'let us do good to all people, especially to … the family of believers' (Galatians 6:10). When people see the love that Christians have for one another, they will see the character of God and be attracted to him. 'By this everyone will know that you are my disciples, if you love one another' (John 13:35). This was a key theme of Jesus' last prayer; it was a passion of the apostles and was exemplified by the early church. Despite these clear instructions there are Christians with AIDS uncared for, Christians in jail unvisited, Christians starving and Christians unloved.

Friendship across cultures

There are numerous opportunities to love people from around the world. Many of us pass in the street people from other countries and cultures on a regular basis. Meeting someone from another country gives you a bridge into their culture. You could start by going out of your way to meet your neighbours from different countries, especially refugees if you have any near you. If you are at school or college then find out about the backgrounds of your classmates. Make an effort to befriend those who are from different cultures. At work, you are bound to come across people from different backgrounds. Does your company have contacts in other countries through its head office or subsidiaries, its suppliers or customers? Are there opportunities for you to meet people from these overseas companies? Or to travel with work?

Developing relationships may require some research into foreign culture. Over the past few years there has been a substantial inflow of Somalis into Streatham, where I live. There is one street near our home where a large number of men (it is all men) stand around to chat and smoke. How can one break into such an apparently tight-knit and alien community? So far we have made some initial enquiries in shops, and met a woman who was delighted to show us round and introduce us to several of the local characters. We were given a warm welcome everywhere and free sweets. We have gone to a Somali cultural evening held in a local church hall as part of the Streatham Festival. In conversations there, it appears that there may be opportunities for my wife to be involved in teaching English to some of the women and children on a voluntary basis. My next step is to find a male friend to go with me to one of the restaurants and see what happens. When we reflect on how hard it is for Westerners to go to Somalia, it is amazing that such a large and vibrant community has appeared on our doorstep.

Hospitality

Our homes are a wonderful base for reaching out to people from other cultures. Consider whether you might host people from overseas visiting your church. Refugees have been much in the news in the UK. Are any living near you? Where do they come from? Is there anything that you can do to serve them? Invite people over, show them love and start to listen to their stories. People have often never been invited into a family home in the country in which they have come to live. Although conversation is sometimes hard work, you will be amazingly enriched by the experience.

When you cook for visitors you can also explore the regions of the world. Most supermarkets have the ingredients for producing meals from numerous regions. As the Alpha course has demonstrated, food is a vital part of relationships. This applies to almost all cultures throughout the world. So what about having a party or meal and inviting a cross-section of friends and strangers from other cultures? Ask them to bring a national dish. Everyone will have a great time and friendships will be formed that will enrich people's lives.

Huge numbers of students come to study in the UK. Many are desperately lonely. If you are a student yourself, look out for people from other countries on your courses and in your halls of residence. For the rest of us, let's open our homes to invite foreign students in for meals. Have you thought of sharing your Christmas with a foreign visitor? If you don't meet any foreign students, then agencies such as Friends International (www.friendsinternational.org.uk) can help put you in touch.

My wife Stella teaches English to a range of foreign students, including refugees, in Lambeth, South London. About twice a year we invite her class back to our home for a meal. Every occasion is different, depending on the mix of ages, nationalities and English ability! But all have been hugely rewarding. We have frequently been overwhelmed by the generosity and gratitude of people who appreciate so much the little that we do. We have also been given some amazing food to try.

Candy and Wendy

Candy and Wendy were two sisters from Costa Rica who stayed with us when they came to London for a conference. They then came back for three months to help improve their English. Through them we got to try Costa Rican coffee and to learn about the issues affecting the church and society in Central America. They also encouraged both our children in speaking Spanish.

What about having people to stay? There are huge opportunities to let rooms to visiting students. As we learn more about other cultures we will be more sensitive to the customs and culture of our guests. Ask questions and let them be your guide. That way you will demonstrate your interest in their culture and religion and learn valuable lessons.

Addressing stigma and the most marginalized

Jesus made efforts to reach out to the most marginalized in his community. He was willing to touch lepers, to speak to women and foreigners and to be associated with prostitutes and tax collectors. By comparison, we often try to avoid association with people whom we feel will damage our reputation, challenge our cultural norms or open us to criticism from others. Who are the marginalized in our communities? Perhaps sex offenders, those with mental illness and those who are HIV positive. How welcome are marginalized people in your church?

HIV is a key test. As we have opportunity, we are called to stand with homosexuals, drug users, rape victims and others who have contracted the virus, whether through ignorance, folly, sin or their inability to control the actions of others who have infected them. Are our attitudes those of stigma or acceptance? The church has the opportunity to show extraordinary love by supporting HIV-positive people within our own communities, many of whom come from countries where the prevalence rate is high.

Our society is also characterized by divisions between religious groups. Relations between Christians and Muslims are vital. Many Muslims in our own nations will have strong links with communities overseas and may be first, second or third generation immigrants. Will you reach out across this divide to make friends with Muslim neighbours? You will often find people who have a shared commitment to addressing the moral and behavioural problems in our communities. Most Muslims that I have met, including my next-door neighbours on both sides, are gentle and friendly, and challenge profoundly the negative stereotypes in our media.

Making contacts overseas

There are many ways that we can also begin to build friendships overseas. People that you know may move to a developing country. Make an effort to keep up with them. Ask friends living overseas about their experiences and the people that they meet. Visits and holidays in both directions give opportunities to make friends. Pen pals may largely be a thing of the past, but the spread of the English language and the advance of the internet have hugely expanded the opportunities to make friendships across borders. You can develop an email friendship with people in far-flung locations. And through friendships we can start to pray for individuals, communities and nations. The fact that you know someone in a country where there is a coup, a famine or an earthquake will make a huge difference to your engagement and response.

Sponsoring a child (or a granny) in a developing country also provides the opportunity to create relationships. Most of these schemes involve letter-writing and the exchange of cards, with the possibility of paying a visit. Inevitably, these relationships can be superficial, but many people have found it a real way into praying for a family, a community and a nation.

Writing to and visiting prisoners

We are told in Hebrews 13:3 to 'remember those in prison as if you were together with them in prison'. That implies prayer, empathy and practical concern. As well as campaigning at a general level for human rights and justice, there are numerous opportunities to befriend prisoners and, where appropriate, to campaign for their release. There has always been a particular Christian role in highlighting the needs of political prisoners, whether Christian or not. In addressing human rights abuses worldwide, we are called to campaign for people being persecuted, whatever their faith. But we should also show particular concern for Christians facing persecution.

Various agencies, such as Amnesty International and Christian Solidarity Worldwide (CSW), campaign for justice and the release of individual prisoners. They would be happy to give you names and addresses of prisoners to write to (see the websites at the end of chapter 9). You can link this to your focus countries and form a direct link. Organizations such as CSW produce a special list for Christmas which gives you and your church the opportunity to send cards to those in prison, including Christians. And there are also foreign prisoners in the UK. Many of these have few visitors and would love to have someone take an interest in them and write to them or visit them.

Prison Fellowship International

The Prison Fellowship was founded in the United States by Charles Colson, who worked for President Nixon and was jailed for his involvement in the Watergate affair. The Prison Fellowship of England and Wales (www.prisonfellowship.org.uk) provides opportunities for Christians and churches to link to their local prisons through letter writing, visiting, leading worship services and Bible studies and providing support to prisoners' families. Their website notes that there are over 6,000 volunteers supporting the chaplaincy service in prisons in England and Wales, showing the important role of the church in prison work.

Writing to prisoners overseas makes a difference. It provides a huge encouragement to the individual, but also highlights to the authorities that they are not forgotten and that someone outside is taking an interest in their case. The challenge is actually doing it. To have lots of good feelings and intentions is not as effective as a single prayer or letter. Why not pray and write right now? Write your address on the letter and there is always the chance that the prisoner may be able to reply. I remember the excitement in our small church when we heard of specific answers to prayer and got a reply from one of the people to whom we had sent Christmas cards. Cards only take a few minutes to write, but mean a great deal to those who receive them.

Subscribe to Christian Solidarity Worldwide's *Response* magazine or a similar publication, and start to write letters on a regular basis to overseas prisoners. Set a target for the number of letters that you will write. If you send one a month, then that builds up to 120 over a decade. How many of those people may find their lives enriched and their release accelerated because of your concern?

Taking action

Try to meet some new people from other countries over the next year. That may mean inviting a foreign student or refugee into your home for a meal. Build on any contact that you make by researching their country in more depth. Add it to your priority list and start to pray and get involved however you can.

One-off actions

- Invite a foreign student or refugee into your home.
- Research the nationalities of people living in your road.
- Subscribe to Friends International.
- Have a party.

Daily/weekly

- Make a commitment to visit someone regularly.
- Develop an email correspondence with someone overseas.

Monthly

- Visit a foreign shop and talk to the people who run it.
- Read a foreign magazine or book, or go to a foreign film.
- Write to a prisoner.

Going deeper

- Sponsor a child or granny.
- Research a local community and get involved.
- Get involved with Prison Fellowship.

Useful websites

- **www.friendsinternational.co.uk**   Friends International is a Christian organization offering friendship to international students during their time in the UK. They seek to encourage and equip churches and individual Christians to befriend some of the estimated 1 million foreign students in the UK at any time. An estimated 600,000 of these are learning English in language schools. Friends International works in over 30 cities across the UK.
- **www.csw.org.uk**   Christian Solidarity Worldwide provides a 'voice for the voiceless' by campaigning on human rights issues, specializing in issues of religious freedom. CSW works on behalf of those persecuted for their Christian beliefs and promotes religious liberty for all. The organization began in 1979 as the UK branch of the Swiss-based organization, Christian Solidarity International. In 1997, it was decided to separate from the founding body and the charity adopted the name Christian Solidarity Worldwide. Since then, a number of like-minded groups from

across the world have begun working together as international Christian Solidarity Worldwide partners.

- For other human rights organizations see the websites listed at the end of chapter 9.

CHAPTER 12

Action 5: Encouraging Other People

We are the people we have been waiting for.   Lisa Sullivan

Lisa Sullivan was an African American woman from Washington DC who campaigned for the rights of black young people. She was a friend of Jim Wallis, who often tells her story and quotes this quote. She died in 1990, aged 32. She was a leader, a positive person who inspired others and was not willing to be put off by the barriers to change. We need people like Lisa to inspire others and attempt the impossible.

I have heard Jim Wallis tell the story of Lisa Sullivan more than once at the Greenbelt festival. Imagine my surprise in the autumn of 2006, returning from Greenbelt to see Lisa's quote on the side of a London bus at my local bus garage in Streatham (see the photos section). It shows how Lisa's example and words live on to inspire others. With modern communications, your example could be the spark for millions of people across the world.

The world does not need more organizations, but it does need a movement of people committed to seeing people released from poverty. That will depend on people speaking out to their friends and encouraging them to get on board. This can be hard work and we often have to strive against the cynicism and lethargy of our society. But if you can show that people can be set free from poverty, and that individuals can play a significant part, then many will respond. People are looking for meaning and to be part of a greater cause, and you can get them involved in this most vital of work.

We all have huge influence with our families, friends and wider networks of contacts at work and in the community. How can we involve them in freeing people from poverty and so multiply our impact?

What the Bible teaches

1. God wants us to encourage one another

> ...encouraging one another – and all the more as you see the Day approaching.
> Hebrews 10:25

Jesus' model was to gather a group around him and mould their lives. 'Come, follow me,' he said (Matthew 4:19). God arranges where we live and who our neighbours are. He gifts us differently for the common good (1 Corinthians 12:7–11).

2. God works though children and families

> From the lips of children and infants you have ordained praise.
> Matthew 21:16

We have particular responsibilities to our own households – to teach our children how they should live (Proverbs 22:6) and to encourage others in our household to follow God. God wants our homes to be places of blessing, and loves to see lonely people welcomed into families (Psalm 68:6).

3. We are called to be leaders and influencers of others

> You are the light of the world. A city on a hill cannot be hidden.
> Matthew 5:14

We are to be salt and light in our workplaces and communities. We are to call others to be disciples, and challenge them to follow Christ and our example, as Paul did (1 Corinthians 11:1).

You have more influence than you think

You may feel that there is not much that you can do, and that you do not have much influence. It's not true. Think about the actions that you have taken, the prayers you have prayed and the money that you have given. Think most of all about the people who look to you as an example: people in your family, at work or in the community. They may be few, but the impact that you have in their lives may be decisive. And for some people you will be the only person who has the opportunity to influence them for the kingdom of God, or to get them involved in the fight against poverty. Pray and believe that God will use you to do that and then step out and see what happens.

Whatever your passion, it will communicate to others. Influencing others can mean things like:

- sharing books and leaflets with people and encouraging them to pray and get involved;
- inviting people to join you on a march; or
- telling people about the changes that you have made and encouraging them to join you.

All of us have more influence than we realize. As we spend time with people, they will catch our lifestyle and see what God is doing in us and through us. Our children, in particular, will catch the vision of what we are passionate about. Much as I might wish to stop supporting Birmingham City Football Club, I can't. I picked up the passion from my dad and have bequeathed it to my son. I will always look for their results and dream that one day they will win a trophy. How much better if we can also inspire our children with a love for Christ and poor people.

We live in a very individualistic society. But real change happens when people start to work together, and you can make a much bigger difference as a church, small group or family. Why not form a group to work through the issues in this book and take action together? The pattern is that as we spend time with people, and become their friends, both they and we are changed. In the New Testament we see how Paul gathered a group of people around him for his missionary journeys. They learned from him and caught the vision of a man who could say: 'Follow my example, as I follow the example of Christ' (1 Corinthians 11:1).

Having an impact in a difficult environment

In some of the countries where Tearfund works, it is not possible for our teams to speak of their faith. But by working alongside Christians, many people have begun to see what the gospel can mean in terms of a life lived in the service of others. We all influence those around us more than they or we realize. I visited the team responding to the Pakistan earthquake in 2005, who lived first in tents for several months and then in converted containers to bring the needed relief to remote countries. Tearfund employed local Muslim people in Kashmir to work on these programmes. Their feedback was of how much they appreciated working for an organization that had clear principles and demonstrated integrity in all its dealings.

Your family and household

Your greatest influence is likely to be with your partner and children, or your housemates. Choosing to watch television programmes about development can be a great conversation starter. You can inject development issues into your family prayer times. You can plan your holidays with a development dimension, get children involved in ethical shopping, or decide together as a family about giving to poorer countries. The possibilities are endless.

Inspiring children is vital. They often have a deep concern for poor people and I have no doubt that God particularly honours their prayers and actions. How do we get children involved? Encourage them in languages, stamps, coin collecting, travel and interest in development issues, and mix in some prayer for the countries concerned. Think about the subjects that they learn at school. If they are learning a foreign language, consider prioritizing a country that speaks that language. Look at what they are learning in geography and history and get excited about the global dimensions. The Olympics and the football World Cup provide a great focus for thinking about various countries around the world, with unique opportunities to meet people from all over the world for those in the host city.

Influencing your family

Tearfund has two volunteers called Heather and Richard Moore. After becoming a Christian in 1978, Heather became aware that Christianity meant more than just attending church and looked for practical ways to be more active, without upsetting her family. She decided to sponsor a nurse and got very interested in the work of Tearfund, becoming a church representative. She also started to pray for her husband and kept it up for twelve years, until he became a Christian in 1990. When he did, he also felt that he needed to do something practical for God, and they both got involved in selling Tearcraft goods produced by poor communities. Richard went on a Tearcraft visit to Bangladesh and Thailand, and vowed that next time he wanted to be able to help. God had equipped him with many practical skills and he volunteered for Tearfund's disaster response teams. He went to Albania to help manage rubbish removal and build hospital incinerators, then Mozambique to help in the flood relief, Sierra Leone digging and cleaning wells and toilets, and Sudan to build toilets in the refugee camps. Heather and Richard are very much a team, working together to reduce spiritual and physical poverty.

A global perspective can affect the TV we watch, the websites we access and the newspapers that we read. Look out for international coverage, especially on the countries that you are ed in. Look for the international dimension of the ... hat interest you; whether this is food or the sports ... hat you support. Check out some of the websites specifically geared towards children and development such as www.schoolaid.tv (World Vision) and http://actionpack.tearfund.org (Tearfund).

Your local community

As you look beyond the household, it is good to think how you can work with others to effect change. What groups are you already part of? Are you in a youth club, a tennis club, or involved with Scouts or Guides? Use those networks to spread the message about global issues and to get people involved. If there is a disaster, why not organize a specific collection within your group, and keep them informed of how progress is being made. Could you encourage your neighbours to get involved with giving to a development project or sponsoring a child together? What local groups are there that care about global issues? Can you get involved?

Working a miracle

In 2006, Tearfund launched an appeal called 'Work a Miracle', encouraging people to give £7 – the amount it costs to help prevent the transmission of HIV from a mother to her child during childbirth. Joanne Pilkington, who works for Tearfund in the East Midlands, had a friend, Alison Hayes, who had the idea of inviting 7 people to a £7 lunch at which she also showed the 'Work a Miracle' DVD. This was copied by several other volunteers, and so Joanne thought she had better try it herself. Being unsure who to invite, she issued an open invitation and ended up with 26 adults, plus children. A number of people who were unable to come also gave a gift and the event raised £262.50, enough to support 37 mothers and their children.

Who lives in your road? In our road in South London we have people from Guyana, Italy, South Africa, Bangladesh, Pakistan, Malawi and probably a few other countries. Even in rural areas, there can be amazing diversity. What local restaurants do you have? We now have Thai, Mexican, Indian, Chinese, Italian, Greek and West Indian all within easy reach. Did you know that most Indian restaurants in the UK are run by Bangladeshis, and that most of them come from the north-eastern district of Sylhet in Bangladesh? Why not ask when you next visit. Even if they are not from there, it is a great way to open a conversation.

Can you engage with other religions in your area? If conflict between religions is to be replaced by dialogue, it needs to happen through numerous local initiatives. In Balham, just down the road from our house, we have, amongst others, a mosque, a Hindu temple and a Polish church and centre. Following the bombings of 2005, there are increasing opportunities for engagement between different faith groups. How about visiting your local mosque? It may also lead to contacts with some key ethnic minority communities.

Coffee and giving

We can also inject a development dimension into our existing societies and groups. Community groups are often strong supporters of charity work. My mother, Judy Grant, was a member of a women's group in Bromsgrove. When that came to an end, the individuals continued to meet for coffee, collecting a pound per person per session, and donated money in £10 units. So far they have given over £600 to charity. How about challenging your local club or society to get involved in supporting a development project in the same way?

How can you help local schools to have a global perspective? If you have children at school, then encourage their teachers to involve development issues in the lessons. For those of you who are teachers, there are excellent resources available from

ıware (www.worldaware.org.uk), now run by the SOS
ɛn's Villages charity, and Global Eye (www.globaleye.
org.uk), run by the Royal Geographical Society. Even if you
aren't a teacher, you may be able to highlight some of these
resources for your children's teachers.

Where you work or study

We spend much of our time at work and form many of our
relationships there. Friends at work may well be interested in
development issues and willing to get involved if you take a
lead. Some companies have schemes for giving away money to
charitable causes. How about volunteering for the committee
that makes decisions about these resources and promoting the
cause of organizations working with poverty and development
issues? Most companies have a staff magazine. Why not write
an article on development issues linked to your company and,
if you travel to a developing country, write a feature and put in
some photos? Offer to do a talk with pictures if that would be
appropriate.

Work is a great place to sell craft goods from poor countries such as the excellent gifts in the Tearcraft catalogue. This
gives revenue to the suppliers and also provides an opportunity to discuss some of the issues around their production.
Friends at work are also often very willing to get involved in
sponsored events. Tearfund staff have been sponsored to run
in the Great South Run. Could you be sponsored for similar
events or even for doing something useful such as decorating
old people's homes, so that you get a double benefit from the
effort?

Getting involved with Non-Governmental Organizations (NGOs)

NGOs, such as Tearfund, are a great channel for your giving and advocacy, but what about more direct involvement? Most organizations are on the lookout for volunteers who will undertake the necessary administration, organization and direct action. The major development NGOs have different strategies on the extent to which they work through regional organizations in the UK. Getting involved with a local group can be a great way to meet like-minded people and increase your knowledge.

The UK is unique in global terms in the strength of its NGOs and public campaigning on poverty issues. This gives us some unique opportunities. The World Bank, when it wants to consult NGOs, usually starts with the UK because of the strength of Oxfam, Christian Aid and others in both their policy analysis and campaigning. By engaging with an NGO you will have opportunity to learn more and to get involved in thinking through policy issues and ideas.

Many charities offer opportunities to be involved in fund-raising and speaking. They may run shops where you could volunteer. This provides opportunities both to raise money and to make contacts in the community, often with poor people, and with like-minded fellow staff. There are many local groups that meet to campaign and get involved in local fairs and carnivals, and other events during the year. It is really encouraging to meet and work together with other people committed to reducing world poverty.

Taking action

The greatest legacy you can leave is the influence that you have had on others. That is why encouraging other people at all levels is such a key factor for the growth of the kingdom of God and the fight against poverty.

One-off actions

- Organize an event around the next Olympics or World Cup.
- Sell Tearcraft at work.
- Invite someone else to join you on a march.
- Find out who lives in your road.

Daily/weekly

- Watch the news with your family.
- Encourage your children to shop for Fairtrade goods.
- Pray for your friends and family to catch your vision.

Monthly

- Buy your children books written in developing countries.
- Watch a TV programme on a development issue with your family.
- Pray for someone else to go on a mission trip.

Going deeper

- Do a sponsored event.
- Have an awayday from work at a social project.
- Get involved with a local NGO.
- Buy this book for someone else.
- Circulate a Tearcraft catalogue at work.

Useful websites

- **www.generous.org.uk**   'A year of living generously' is a brilliant site which 1,500 people have got together to commit themselves to a range of small actions, from turning off taps to becoming an organ donor, in order to make the world a better place. Over 8,000 actions have been taken so far, and counting...

- **www.christianaid.org.uk**   Christian Aid has a strong capacity in research and advocacy. Through focused campaigns on issues such as trade, climate change and corruption, they have been able to combine strong research, which has influenced the policy debate, with popular messages that have helped to mobilize supporters.

- **www.relationaltithe.com**   Relational Tithe is a global community trying to live out God's economy of abundance and generosity. Their key themes are relationships and redistribution. They are seeking to rediscover in a radical way what can happen when Christians form new economic structures through pooling their tithes and giving directly to those in need. This is still at an early stage but it looks like it will grow and expand worldwide.

CHAPTER 13

Action 6: Mobilizing Your Church

We must stand up against evil. There is a prophetic side to the church. Pius Ncube, Archbishop of Bulawayo, Zimbabwe
(at a meeting with Tearfund, November 2006)

I met Pius Ncube, the Roman Catholic Archbishop of Bulawayo, when he came to London in November 2006. He is a small and serious man, with a steely determination to stand for justice and against oppression. He asked for prayer for hope, and to overcome the depression of ordinary people in Zimbabwe. He stressed the priority of supporting women's groups in the country and the importance of foreign governments and the European Union keeping up the pressure on the Zimbabwean government to uphold human rights. As I listened, I was struck in part by his clear and courageous criticism of the Zimbabwean Government and President, but also by his sadness and anger at the division in the churches. Rather than standing side by side to oppose the Government, the churches were divided and compromised, partly by Government infiltration.

Since the time of that meeting Pius Ncube has been subject to a Government campaign against him and was forced to resign in 2007. Many churches in Zimbabwe, however, have also been taking an increasingly courageous stand, speaking out to the Government on behalf of poor communities. They see this as a central part of their commitment to bring God's word to their society, and complementary to their work to support AIDS orphans and promote food security. In the midst of the suffering in Zimbabwe, God is building a church that reflects his heart for justice, and for poor and lost people.

Our churches need to change radically, to be converted so that we care for poor and oppressed people and not our own comfort. God intends his church to be courageous in its stand against evil and to show the world what a redeemed and loving community can look like. We are called to imitate Jesus in his passion for the lost, the sick and the suffering. The quality of the life of the church and the extent to which it demonstrates the character of God are much more important than whether we are popular or powerful. How is your church doing?

What the Bible teaches

1. The local church is the hope of the world

> *You are a chosen people ... that you may declare the praises of him who called you out of darkness.*   1 Peter 2:9

The church is God's instrument to reach the world with his love (Acts 13:1–3). The New Testament church overflowed with love and generosity to poor people. God gifts and equips his church to serve and be generous (2 Corinthians 9:9). We have the spiritual and physical resources to meet the needs of our communities and the world. The New Testament gives examples of churches serving poor people and giving gifts. Jesus laid down his life for us, and we are called to model sacrificial love and service (1 John 3:16).

2. We are called to honour poor people in our churches

> *Suppose someone comes into your meeting wearing a gold ring and fine clothes and a poor person in filthy old clothes also comes in.*   James 2:2

The church is the community in which God breaks down the divisions between rich and poor, old and young, slave and free (Galatians 3:28). The church must be a place where poor people are welcomed and made at home (James 2:3–4). The true measure of our religion is how we treat the weak. God expects us to look after widows and orphans in their distress (James 1:27).

3. The church must teach the right things

> *Command those who are rich ... to be generous and*
> *willing to share.* 1 Timothy 6:17–18

Our actions are driven by our theology. It is vital that the church is shaped by biblical teaching, including teaching in relation to poor people (2 Timothy 1:13–14). The church should be challenging people to live simply and sacrificially. It must be prophetic to challenge the evils of the world, including consumerism and greed, and to uphold God's values for relationships, power and money (1 John 2:15).

Is your church bringing good news to poor people?

In the last chapter, we spoke about getting involved with others and multiplying our influence through family, friends and colleagues. But what about the church? I believe that the local church is God's primary instrument to change the world. This will happen both through direct action in local communities and through a global network concerned about poverty and human rights.

In many parts of the world the church is already present as a transformed and transforming community of God. When it works well, a church can be the place where poor people are affirmed in their value and gifting, and rich people are enabled to find humility and to use their resources in the service of others. Local churches are, by their very nature, based on relationships and local knowledge. Through integral mission, they can bring the hope of the gospel in both its spiritual and physical dimensions to the communities which they serve.

In other places the church is siding with the rich and powerful and is deaf to the voice of poor people. What is your church like? Are you serving poor people in your community and around the world? What do your publicity materials say about your welcome to people of all backgrounds? Churches can reach out across cultural boundaries, and become a venue for refugee clubs and drop-in centres. They can provide a powerful focus for most of the actions in this book including giving, campaigning, prayer and lifestyle change. Will your church rise to this challenge and become one of the 100,000? By inspiring your church to have a passion for poor people, you can multiply hugely your personal impact.

You could start by working with others to assess the current impact of your church. Just as you did stock-taking as an individual, you can do so as a church. What activities and links do you have? The church needs to understand its own area, and to be involved with serving poor people locally. It is enormously helpful to do a research project on the local area, highlighting spiritual and physical needs, and cultural diversity. Consider how you can serve people and make contacts by, for example, organizing joint activities with other churches or arranging visits to other religious groups.

Globally you can document the countries that people in your congregation come from or have links to. What missionaries and organizations do you support? Have you thought of volunteering to take responsibility for coordinating mission or prayer work in your church? You could be the person to inject a world and integral mission perspective into your church's prayer life. By praying for different countries, mission partners and countries in the news, the whole church can gradually become more aware of global challenges and opportunities.

I was struck in Tanzania that, even amongst lively

churches which were full of the Holy Spirit and God's word, there was a huge difference between those with an inward and those with an outward focus. The former seemed most keen on using their resources on church buildings and facilities, and employing full-time workers. The latter were concerned about how they could serve poor people outside the church. It was the outward-looking churches that inspired hope and excitement. The same is true in the West.

Christian development agencies must support the local church

The church is central to God's plan, and the local church in particular is the means that he uses to change communities. Church denominations and specialist Christian development and mission organizations must support the work of the local church and not marginalize it. Christian development agencies face a choice as to whether they work through or around the local church. If in ten years' time we have strengthened our own organizations to serve poor people, but left local churches weak and marginalized, then we will not have contributed to God's long-term strategy.

Challenges facing the church

Churches need to recognize that serving poor people is part of their core ministry. This is not something that distracts them from preaching the gospel, but it is one of the strongest manifestations of the gospel, modelled on the life and ministry of Jesus. The local church should be at the centre of integral mission.

All too often, churches have been selfish in enjoying their own blessings, and not sensitive to the needs of the world. Reflect on your own church's priorities. Your church needs to be realistic about its attitudes and actions and to repent of areas where it is not living up to its calling. That means identifying and addressing the obstacles that your church faces in serving poor people. My list is as follows:

Materialism

One of the barriers for rich churches to be committed to integral mission is an obsession with their own programmes and financial needs. Many Western churches benefit from resources and levels of material comfort unknown to most communities throughout the world. Is your church taking poverty seriously or spending most of its time, energy and money on itself? Can you match up to the church I saw in Sao Paulo which is meeting in a tent so that its resources are not diverted from serving poor people to be spent on church buildings?

Lack of unity

We are often divided as a church. There is, for example, little contact between churches from the different ethnic groups in the UK. A visible demonstration of our unity in Christ would provide a prophetic sign to the world. We would also benefit from more cross-fertilization with churches that have different links with poor countries. We must work together.

Alignment with political powers

Our closeness to governments and the rich and powerful has often blunted our commitment to poor people. From the imperial powers of Rome, through subsequent empires and up to the present day, the desire of the church to be accepted by the state has led to a lack of compassion for the oppressed and a lack of passion for mission. We need to be radical in our commitment to poor and oppressed people.

Poor theology

We must challenge the dualism that separates individual salvation from the need to address poverty and injustice. Evangelical Christians in the West have been guilty of this in the past, but for some churches there has been a real change over the past thirty years. The impact of the 'prosperity gospel', however, is far reaching, particularly in Africa, and there is a major task to introduce the concept of integral mission into the teaching of the church worldwide.

Is the prosperity gospel biblical?

The Bible gives us lots of promises that if we obey and trust in God, then we will be blessed. In Old Testament times this often meant physical blessings. In the New Testament there are numerous warnings to Christians against seeking wealth. Paul says that if we have food and clothing, we should be content with that (1 Timothy 6:8). Jesus demonstrated a voluntary giving up of all the riches of heaven to serve poor and needy people on earth. We are called to do the same. The prosperity gospel takes us away from the servant heart of Christ towards self-fulfilment and greed. In Guatemala, I saw the influence of televangelists and their prosperity gospel message on the church. By bringing an exclusive focus on personal salvation and blessing, such preaching risks cutting the church off from the urgent needs of poor people within society. The prosperity gospel is not biblical.

Lack of love to outsiders

We are often not welcoming to those who are different from us. It is extraordinary how often people just talk to their own friends in church. God calls us to be sensitive to the needs of the marginalized, and if people don't even find a welcome at our services, then we have a major problem. We need to love outsiders.

Inadequate national voice

Churches don't speak out enough at a national level. Our leaders have not been able to get national prominence for the church's commitment to poverty reduction and we need to find both ordinary Christians and high-level advocates who can bring these messages to the centre of national debate. The church needs to take a lead in campaigning on poverty and justice issues.

Autocratic leadership

Dominant leaders can limit the engagement of ordinary church people in integral mission and restrict the extent to which the church is able to be a welcoming and supportive community.

What kind of church will yours be? I pray that it will become a church characterized by simplicity, unity, radical commitment, biblical teaching, love and a voice for poor people. For most, there will be a big agenda to address in mobilizing your church to act in this way. But there is also a huge amount of goodwill and activism already there. Sometimes it is just a matter of someone taking the initiative.

Church mobilization

How can churches be changed? Tearfund uses the phrase 'church mobilization' to describe a process by which churches draw on biblical teaching to become convinced of God's calling to serve poor people, and are then transformed to take action. We have seen this work in the UK through an extended process of biblical learning and action called 'Church, Community and Change'. This has been effective in leading churches into a new commitment to serve their communities. A more accessible version of this course, known as Discovery, is now available and being taken forward in Liverpool and Glasgow, amongst other places. We have seen a comparable process of church and community mobilization working dramatically in East Africa, and also in Asia and Latin America, where churches have been transformed in a way that has not only seen them serving the spiritual and physical needs of poor people in their communities, but also growing in worship and discipleship.

All Nations Church, Clapham Park, London

All Nations was my church for many years prior to going to Bangladesh in 1992. In 1988 my pastor, Les Ball, was approached by a friend from Operation Mobilisation who suggested that he might go to India. Les was traditional, had never even been to France, and was uncomfortable with foreign food. Sensing God's call, however, he went to Bihar in India. Since then he has ministered in Uganda, Zambia, Central Asia, Norway, Germany, the Czech Republic, Bangladesh, the Gambia and Malawi. The church has developed strong links with church-planting work in Bihar. Numerous teams have gone out to visit, giving individuals a chance to experience the challenges of church planting and community work in India at first hand. The church is now decked out with flags from all over the world and has become a completely multi-cultural congregation.

Equally significant has been the stream of visitors to All Nations Church, including Masih Das, a pastor from Bihar whose humility and love have had a profound impact on the church. His evangelistic ministry is now supported by All Nations and deep bonds have developed between the churches in India and London.

Worship, teaching and finances in the church

Your image of God in worship has a powerful influence on your behaviour. Worship that focuses on the intimacy of your relationship with God will nourish your spirituality, but may give less impetus to your service in the world. Many songwriters, including Tim Hughes and Andy Flanagan, are writing songs focused on the character of God as a God of justice and compassion – the God of the poor. As you worship through these songs, God will stir your heart to serve poor people.

In the same way, those who draw up the teaching and preaching programmes of your church have a huge influence. Why not have a series of sermons on justice issues and seek to integrate them into small-group studies? There are excellent Bible study materials for small groups, and our discipleship programmes should include teaching on integral mission. More recently, there has been the development of various courses which highlight biblical teaching on poverty and justice issues and provide practical opportunities for service. Why not run one of these, such as, Just People? The Micah course, at your church? (See www.tearfund.org for more details.) You can use the festivals of the church to highlight the needs of the wider world. Many organizations produce excellent materials for Easter and harvest. You can also have a slot in services from time to time to share news of campaigns and of the needs of the world, and to pray.

Your Sunday school can help children to develop a knowledge of, and love for, the world. They can learn to see prayers answered and to link their own lives with those of children elsewhere in the world. God speaks to many people at a very early age. God called one missionary we knew in Bangladesh when she was eight years old. And as young people grow older, your youth work needs to give them a vision so that they can make a positive difference in the world.

How is your church budget set? Churches can set a pattern for their members by prioritizing support for people in poverty, both at home and overseas, ahead of their own needs. Many churches choose to 'tithe' their own income by giving away 10 per cent or more to other organizations, especially those involved in mission and poverty reduction.

Church-to-church links

Many churches in the West have links with churches in developing countries, often through a missionary or a personal connection of someone in the congregation. Linking with a church in a developing country can be an exciting process. If both churches are seeking to serve poor people in their own communities, then there are lessons to be shared and the possibility of real partnership. A key factor is to send your pastor, minister or vicar overseas to catch the vision. If he or she has never been to a developing country, then the experience can be life changing. Why not offer to go with them?

There are many pitfalls for the unwary in making direct contacts with developing countries. Costs can be high and resources misdirected. A friend from Malawi spoke of individuals who make a living out of writing to churches in the West with fictitious projects and waiting for the cheques to arrive with minimum accountability. Some interventions, however well meant, can do damage, especially in conflict situations, by bringing resources to the wrong people or in the wrong way. Trusted intermediaries can be invaluable in such cases.

Specialist Christian organizations, including missionary societies, development agencies and other groups, exist to allow churches to engage in a deeper way than would otherwise be possible. Such different approaches should be complementary. It is unclear whether increasing direct contacts are reducing support for traditional agencies. The best vision is where the two can work together, since there will be much for churches seeking to embark on such partnerships to learn from those who have been working on these issues for a long period.

Wisley with Pyrford links to Uganda

The parish of Wisley with Pyrford in Surrey has three churches with a growing commitment to global mission and poverty reduction. Neil and Helen Lambert and their family joined the church when Neil was appointed as curate. The Lamberts brought with them a wealth of relationships in Uganda where they had been undertaking church-based development work. In the summer of 2005, eighteen people from the parish in Surrey visited Kasese District in Western Uganda for the first time. They worked with children in six schools and visited orphanages and villages. They left a small gift of money for the church. In summer 2006, four of the original team went back to deepen relationships, and find out how the money had been used. They found that parents of the primary school children had contributed their own resources and labour, and had built new classrooms. A gift of football kit had encouraged young players, some of whom had participated at national level. Healthy goats and chickens were helping to feed the families of widows and orphans. Three communities had been provided with clean water. Eight women's groups had been formed and were being trained in microfinance. The team were amazed at the progress that had been made by people inspired to work together, and supported by small amounts of money. The team reflected: 'People we met in Kasese District were so welcoming and joyful, truly sharing the love of Jesus, and what little they had, with one another.' (For more detail go to www.hopeforuganda.org.uk.)

For the church in Wisley with Pyrford, the key to involvement was firstly to have the courage to move out of their 'comfort zone' into a place where trusting God and their neighbour became essential, and secondly the building of relationships with brothers and sisters in Uganda. Receiving hospitality, and forming genuine, trusting friendships has meant that there is now an ongoing commitment from those in the church to those in Kasese, with people in both countries learning from, and praying for, one another.

Taking action

To mobilize your church, you will need to work both with the leaders and with other members. You will need to be open to opportunities to inject poverty issues into prayers, sermons and Sunday school as you have opportunity. It is a good idea to join any teams responsible for mission or poverty and justice issues. They will probably be a group of committed people who share your passion. Why not give them a copy of this book? And be humble in your prayers and attitudes. Find ways to increase your church's involvement in development issues and to commit yourself to practical service to help make this happen.

One-off actions

- Highlight mission issues in a sermon or Sunday school.
- Offer to lead a section in a prayer meeting.
- Take church members to a development rally or meeting.

Daily/weekly

- Pray for other church members involved in serving.

Monthly

- Provide regular prayer material for church meetings.
- Visit another local church and make some friends.

Going deeper

- Encourage your vicar, minister or pastor to go overseas.
- Join your overseas mission committee.

- Run a Just People? Micah Course at your church or with a group of local churches.
- Develop a church-to-church link.

Useful websites

- www.tearfund.org/tilz   The Tilz site is Tearfund's international learning zone where you can find 18 years' worth of development experience captured on over 8,000 pages. Go to the 'Topics' page and click on 'Church and development', and you will find a range of resources including a Tearfund guide to church mobilization.
- http://en.micahnetwork.org   The Micah Network is the key global group of agencies that is working with issues related to integral mission through the local church. As well as the content of the website, including a section on worship in an integral mission context, you will also find links to other related resources and organizations.
- www.transformationteam.org   Glasgow's Transformation Team works with a wide range of faith communities seeking to overcome poverty in the city. One of the initiatives that it supports is Tearfund's 'Discovery', working with churches in some of the poorest parts of the city. The Transformation Team provides support and training for groups seeking to find funding and practical advice for community projects.

CHAPTER 14

Action 7: Living Simply

Only by God's grace, and with great effort, can we escape the shower of luxuries which has almost suffocated our Christian compassion.

Ronald J. Sider, Rich Christians in an Age of Hunger
(Hodder & Stoughton, 1977, p. 151)

Rich Christians held a mirror up to rich Western Christians in the 1970s and dared to ask whether our lifestyles were consistent both with the gospel and the reality of world poverty. It provoked a range of initiatives for more simple living. Steve Bradbury, the Head of TEAR Australia, recalls the radical impact that the book had upon him as a teacher in Auckland. After reading the book, he and his wife Chris, along with several other members of his small local church, committed themselves to living more simply. The money that they saved went into a 'Zacchaeus Fund', of which 75 per cent was given to EFICOR, a Christian development agency in India, and 25 per cent was retained to meet the needs of poor people in their own community, forcing them to discover the nature and extent of those needs.

The major false god of our age is that of consumerism. We have to challenge the belief that happiness is found in greater consumption – the madness of materialism. It has led to luxury, indulgence and debt in rich countries, while poverty continues to blight the lives of millions of people. The church as a whole has not sustained its commitment to simplicity, and more recently this emphasis appears to have declined in mainstream evangelical Christianity as our standards of living have continued to rise. Living simply is less influential globally than the so-called 'prosperity gospel' that teaches the opposite. Economic inequality between nations has widened over the past thirty years, and the need for the church to demonstrate a different way of living has become even more urgent.

There is a long Christian tradition of emphasizing simplicity. This is not a negative emphasis on giving things up, but a joyful and positive one about how we can use our resources more effectively and equitably to set other people free from poverty. The church has a key role to play in helping society as a whole to find a way towards just and sustainable lifestyles. The world needs to see a community that is living more simply so that others can benefit from the resources that we save. Who else other than the church is going to provide a lead on this?

What the Bible teaches

1. We need to be content

> *Godliness with contentment is great gain.*   1 Timothy 6:6

We are not to live like the world does. As Christians we should not be seeking to maximize our own income, consumption or satisfaction (1 Timothy 6:9). The Bible encourages us to ask for enough for ourselves, our daily bread, while being generous to others. There is no record of Jesus buying anything, but he was happy to benefit from the generosity of friends. Wealth in the Bible is seen as a blessing, a responsibility and a potential snare (Proverbs 11:28). The ideal is for those who have wealth to use it voluntarily to benefit poor people (1 Timothy 6:18).

2. People must come before profits

> *Seek first his kingdom and his righteousness.*
> Matthew 6:33

Even if they seem distant, we are in relationship with those we trade with. We must not deprive poor people of just wages. A person's cloak is to be returned even if taken in pledge, so that he or she will not be cold at night (Deuteronomy 24:12–13). Provision is to be made for poor people within economic enterprises, so that there is not profit maximization but a deliberate provision for those in need. We must pay a living wage to workers. There should be a strong emphasis on sharing within the family and nation to ensure that no one suffers economic hardship (Acts 4:34–35).

3. We should loan money to poor people without expecting a return

> ... *if you lend to those from whom you expect repayment, what credit is that to you?*   Luke 6:34

When we bless poor people we bless God. In the New Testament, money is a major theme of Jesus' teaching and source of illustrations for his parables (Matthew 18:21–35). The epistles teach about generosity and this is extended to gifts of love between churches (Romans 15:26). God is honoured as the needs of poor people are met and the earth is protected.

Your income and spending

What is the source of your income – your efforts or God's provision? Do you own what you have, or is it yours on trust? The answers to these questions will hugely affect your actions. Contrary to the advertising message that 'you've earned it, you deserve it', the Bible argues that your wages are ultimately a gift from God. In a market economy we are paid according to supply and demand. Much of this is an accident of location and history. People doing the same jobs in different countries and at different times in history have been paid very different amounts. Nurses in Zambia earn about £100 per month. How do you compare with them in terms of effort and wages?

How much will you earn and spend in your lifetime? A person earning the current average UK national wage of £25,000 for a period of 40 years, and then getting a minimum pension for 20 years, will earn at least £1.1 million and spend about £1 million over their lifetime. What will you spend your income on, and what will be the impact on poverty and the lives of poor people?

Jesus challenged the rich young ruler, for his own benefit, to sell his possessions and give to the poor. Are we confident that we don't face the same barriers to faith that he did? A big test of our discipleship is whether we are willing to live more simply and see a major transfer of our wealth and income to those poorer than ourselves. To be a follower of Jesus, who became poor that we might be rich, is to sacrifice ourselves and our own comfort for the benefit of others. To do so we will need a positive vision of what our money can achieve.

Changing our lifestyles will be a prophetic witness to our generation of what God requires. It will be tough in our culture, but it will also bring us great joy and freedom. A church that is willing to live more simply will be a church that has the opportunity to live the gospel and change the world.

How do we live more simply? It means sitting down with our monthly budget and making decisions on what we can do without. Living simply is not about never having luxuries or celebrating or sharing with others. It is about recognizing that in a culture dominated by spending on ourselves, we all have numerous opportunities to substitute greater generosity for greater consumption. It may mean simpler food, taking sandwiches to work for lunch, cancelling a cable TV subscription or buying new clothes or shoes less frequently.

One encouragement is to put aside the cash when you make a saving so that you can see the impact. Steve Bradbury told me the story of an elderly lady in Tasmania who gave regularly to her church, but also had a 'treats jar'. Every time that she had a treat (chocolate biscuits rather than plain; a trip to an Aussie Rules football game) she would put the same amount as she had spent into the jar to give away. This wasn't stopping her enjoying these extras, but limiting her consumption through a self-imposed tax that also allowed her to be more generous to poor people.

If you want to try out living simply, how about taking a month or two as a trial period? Many churches already have Lent as an ideal focus, but any time would do. You could aim to use up the food that you have in the house, to walk or cycle instead of driving your car, to sacrifice meals out and maybe invite people in instead. How much money could you save? What kind of difference could that make in a developing country?

Living more simply is hard to sustain on your own. It is easier as part of a community. That doesn't have to mean living together, but does mean having deeper economic relationships with each other. Churches are ideal places for that. Major items of equipment can be shared. Resources can be given to poor people without the complications of personal obligation. It can start with just you and a friend. Then seek together to find or create a like-minded local group. Best of all, start to persuade others in your church or Bible study group to get involved and start living differently.

Buying from developing countries

We are all part of a globalized economy. Money comes to us and flows out from us, and if we live simply, invest ethically and give generously, then we can help to make the world more just. As well as our level of spending, we need to think about how we spend our money. Trade is essential for large parts of the world to work their way out of poverty. Buying products made in Sri Lanka or the Philippines can give a boost to employment and exports in those countries. If you want to reduce world poverty, then it makes sense to buy things that are produced by developing countries.

The world trading system

A fair and open world trading system has benefits for everyone. World trade rules are negotiated by national governments at the World Trade Organisation in Geneva. In theory it is one member, one vote, but the rich countries have traditionally dominated these discussions and pursued their own interests, sometimes at the expense of poorer countries. More recently both the poorest and the middle-income developing countries have begun to take a stronger line in the negotiations. The current round of negotiations is meant to be benefiting developing countries, but is going very slowly and seems to hold out little benefit for the poorest countries. At the same time the rich countries, including the USA and the European Union, are negotiating bilateral agreements with individual and regional groupings of developing countries. There is a major concern that by the time the next round of global agreements is finalized, it will have been bypassed by a plethora of individual arrangements in which the power imbalance between rich and poor is far greater.

The availability of goods from developing countries in our markets depends on global trade rules. The biggest impact you can have on helping developing countries exports and economic growth is probably to campaign for fairer trade rules and for global agreements that will help the poorest countries. That means urging richer countries to eliminate the tariffs, or taxes, that they charge on imports from developing countries, and to limit the other restrictions that they often apply. Rich countries also need to eliminate subsidies, particularly on agricultural exports, that make it harder for developing countries to compete in world markets. To get more involved in these issues and to join a campaign, go to the Trade Justice Movement website at www.tjm.org.uk.

The issue of whether poorer countries should also reduce their own tariffs on imports is a hugely contentious one. There is no doubt that it makes consumers better off, including the poorest, to the extent that they buy imported food or goods. But reducing tariffs too quickly can bring damage to developing countries where domestic industries are destroyed by foreign competition and small-scale farmers are undercut by cheap, often subsidized agricultural imports.

Ethical consumerism

As well as buying your goods from developing countries as much as you can, you should also seek to ensure, as far as possible, that your spending is ethical. You should avoid companies who are exploiting their workers or who rely on child labour. If goods are very cheap, you could check with retailers that they are not being produced through abusive practices. This is hard to do for small shops, but the larger retail chains are increasingly open about their buying policies and ethical standards, and you should encourage them to publish as much information as possible. You should avoid companies that are involved in the support of repressive regimes, the arms trade or the production of harmful products such as pornography or cigarettes. Consumers collectively can make choices that persuade producers to support decent working conditions and encourage the ethical sourcing of materials.

Excellent guides are now available which highlight the background of different companies' production and sourcing policies, so that you can make informed choices. To gain access to these sources, I suggest that you start with a book called *The Rough Guide to Ethical Shopping* by Duncan Clark and with the *Ethical Consumer* magazine and website (www.ethicalconsumer.org).

Companies producing in poor countries must safeguard the health and safety of their workers. Some conditions and practices, such as bonded labour (a form of slavery) or unsafe exposure to chemicals, are unacceptable in any context. In such cases, we should not buy the product, but should we do more? This is an area where we can consider lobbying of companies, using our role as consumers or shareholders. As a last resort, consumer boycotts, in which you seek to persuade others not to buy the relevant products, can be effective in highlighting the issues and changing behaviour, but must be based on credible evidence.

Low wages, if they are above subsistence levels, do not in themselves constitute abuse of workers. It is reasonable that companies should pay the going wage in any given country, even if this seems low by Western standards. Low wages attract investment and give the opportunity for employment. Productivity is relatively low in most developing countries, and to insist on high wages is to insist that jobs will move elsewhere. It is a big responsibility to suggest that consumers should boycott goods from a certain country or company. Campaigns in the West that lead to reduced purchases can mean instant dismissal without compensation for vulnerable workers without other sources of income. When faced with apparent abuses, we have to dig deeper and consider the facts of the case in the context of the general standards in the country concerned and whether the company's presence is making things better or worse.

Several commodities now have voluntary labelling schemes that guarantee good practice. The 'Rug Mark' demonstrates that child labour has not been used in the production of carpets. Similar marks exist for sustainable wood and paper, and for fairly traded goods, including footballs. You can choose to shop with organizations that are committed to developing sustainable businesses with good working practices in the poorest countries. These include a range of organizations that market gifts supplied by producers in developing countries within a framework of ethical and sustainable practices (see, for example, the Tearcraft range at www.tearcraft.org).

Fairtrade

Fairtrade provides an opportunity to spend well and ethically. It guarantees a consistent price, usually above world market prices, to farmers and other producers. This reflects Old Testament concepts of justice by being linked to the income required by producers for a decent standard of living, with an additional supplement for investing in social projects.

Fairtrade is not just about poverty, but also about vulnerability to shocks. Perhaps the biggest benefit of Fairtrade arrangements is that they provide a measure of long-term income security for farmers. Poor farmers can face severe fluctuations in world market prices, especially for primary products. The entry of Vietnam into the global coffee market precipitated dramatic price falls, for which African smallholders could not have prepared themselves, and which plunged many into debt and poverty.

Is it more effective to buy Fairtrade than buying the equivalent non-Fairtrade goods at lower prices and then giving away the difference? Almost certainly. Fairtrade targets poor producers and enables them to continue in productive employment. Aid projects will find it very difficult to replicate this impact at similar cost, because Fairtrade builds on the strength of the market, and encourages farmers and other producers to do what they are good at, rather than to rely on handouts.

Buying Fairtrade products will generally cost you more. In doing so, however, you are both providing direct support to producers and modelling a different way to live other than by pure market economics. Fairtrade models a biblical pattern where profit maximization is not the only objective. It restores some element of personal relationship back into trade. As Fairtrade expands, we can use our daily shopping more and more to help change the way the world does business. If you find Fairtrade too expensive for your budget, then start gradually with some of the products which are most competitive, such as bananas.

The range of Fairtrade products has been growing rapidly and now numbers over 2,500 in the UK. You can catch up with the latest by visiting the Fairtrade Foundation website at www.fairtrade.org.uk. It is now possible to buy Fairtrade consistently for tea, coffee, bananas, cereal bars and jams, and occasionally for wine, chocolate, clothing and many other items. Supermarkets have responded to public demand by creating their own brand of Fairtrade products.

Ben Clowney: Fairtrade man

During Fairtrade Fortnight 2007, Ben Clowney lived exclusively on Fairtrade products for two weeks. By recording his progress on the MySpace website he brought the issues of Fairtrade to a wider audience and got some great encouragement from well-wishers (see www.myspace.com/fairtrademan). He said that frying muesli in red wine was the lowest moment, but he survived. As well as his diet, which included a lot of rice and dried fruit, he took various actions such as lobbying the G8 Presidency and writing to his local supermarket to ask them to stock more Fairtrade products. I also very much enjoyed the video of him tucking into a steak at the end of the two weeks...

Ethical tourism

One high-profile area of ethical consumerism is that of ethical tourism. Travel to developing countries has expanded hugely over the past twenty years. There are some difficult dilemmas here. The air travel that this has generated raises issues on global warming that we will consider in the next chapter. Tourism provides economic opportunities, but also potential damage to poor communities and fragile ecosystems. Tourism has become a major outlet for luxury spending – resources that could be used much more effectively to reduce poverty in other ways. At the same time, tourism is the main foreign exchange earner for over a third of developing countries.

As part of living more simply, each of us has to decide before God how much we are willing to spend on holidays. Once we have made this decision, however, there are a host of other issues about where we travel to, and how we plan the details of our trips. Our holidays are one way in which we engage directly with people and communities in developing countries. In making travel plans, we can consider options that take account of both environmental and developmental effects. You should try to learn from and respect the cultures that you visit, to inject the maximum amount of resources into local economies, and to ensure that you do no harm.

In some cases we have the chance to make such choices within a given budget. In others, ethical tourism will cost more. The first step is always good information. Tourism Concern publishes *The Ethical Travel Guide*, and their website at www.tourismconcern.org.uk provides a wealth of information. The travel sections of national newspapers, especially the *Guardian* and the *Independent*, now feature a range of eco-tourism articles. To take this further, search for 'responsible tourism' or 'ecotourism' on the internet, or contact the Association of Independent Tour Operators (IATO), which has guidelines to promote responsible tourism. Consider booking through North South Travel (www.northsouthtravel.co.uk), which donates its profits to development work.

In general, countries want tourists. After the 2004 tsunami, one of the best responses to help suffering locations was to go back as a tourist and spend money. But there is a huge difference between staying in an internationally owned hotel and consuming imported products where the benefits to the local economy are likely to be largely through staff wages, and a more developmentally friendly option where hotels and restaurants source as many goods as possible from the local economy, develop and train local staff and re-invest in the economy.

The pros and cons of being a tourist

On the positive side, tourism can create employment, with up to two staff for every guest in some resorts. Income from tourism can support local businesses and provide resources to invest in development. Las Marias in Honduras has used tourist revenue to improve its sanitation system and dramatically reduce illness in the local population. On the negative side, tourists can take the lion's share of scarce water resources. An 18-hole golf course can use as much water as a town of 10,000 people. Forests can be felled to make way for hotels, swimmers can destroy coral reefs and local people can be evicted to make way for tourist facilities. Choosing carefully can make a real difference to the impact of your holiday.[14.1]

Ethical finance, savings and investment

The way we manage our finances, including banking, borrowing, saving, investing, insurance and pensions, can have a powerful impact on world poverty. Your bank account contributes to the high profits earned by retail banks, and may finance investments by your bank in companies and countries that you would not support (see www.banktrack.org). Have you considered moving your current account and credit cards to an ethical bank such as the Co-operative Bank, or Smile, its internet banking offshoot?

Income in the world is unfairly distributed, but wealth even more so. The few richest people in the world have enormous wealth, while many poor individuals and countries are in debt. Private debt has also been expanding rapidly in richer countries. Average household debt in the UK now stands at about £9,000.[14.2] Dealing with debt in the church and wider society is a vital first step for many people before they can take control of their finances and be generous givers. Christians Against Poverty is a Tearfund partner which provides practical Christian help to those struggling with their own personal debt, and Rob Parsons' book *The Money Secret* is warmly recommended as a way into the issues.

Shared Interest

Shared Interest is a UK-based co-operative lending society that aims to reduce poverty in the world, by providing fair and just financial services. Members of Shared Interest invest money which is lent to companies in developing countries. They are offered a low rate of interest (1 per cent when I looked at the site). Investments are for a minimum of £100 and a maximum of £20,000. Shared Interest is not a specifically Christian organization. It was started in 1990 and has around 8,400 members who have invested more than £20 million. It uses the pooled savings of its members to facilitate business development and trade for poor people. Shared Interest works with Fairtrade businesses all over the world, both producers and buyers, providing credit to enable producers to be paid in advance and to help Fairtrade develop. Shared Interest is owned and controlled by its membership. See www.shared-interest.com.

If you are not in debt, then you are likely to have some savings. How can you use them to make a difference in the world while still preserving them for your future needs? A key to poverty reduction is creating sustainable private businesses that will generate wealth in poorer countries. Many developing countries are characterized by a lack of access to investment funds for small businesses. Schemes now exist for you to invest with varying degrees of risk in funds that will be re-invested to benefit poor people. If you do not need quick access to your money or a high rate of return, then here is a way to benefit others while still preserving your capital for the future. Why not investigate and see if your savings can help create sustainable jobs in poor countries and free people from poverty, through a scheme such as Shared Interest?

Monitoring your pension scheme

For most people, the biggest amount of saving that they have is in their pension scheme. Public sector pensions are generally funded from taxation, but most other pensions are invested and provide a huge source of funds for global economic development. Do you know where your money is invested? My personal pension gives a choice between investing in ethical or general funds. By making that choice I am influencing the investment of more money than I am ever likely to have to invest myself.

Taking action

Action requires you to look at your regular spending and see whether you can live more simply and move towards using more of your income to support poor producers and Fairtrade products. There are also one-off actions involved in assessing your pension scheme and reviewing your own assets to see if you can move any of them into funds that would help support Third World businesses.

One-off actions

- Check out your pension scheme to ensure it is invested ethically.
- Plan your next year's holiday on a lower-cost and more ethical basis.
- Set up a giving jar.
- Analyse your budget to see what you are spending money on.
- Consider moving your current account or savings to an ethical bank.

Daily/weekly

- Buy Fairtrade coffee, tea, bananas and chocolate.
- Buy more from developing countries.
- Borrow and lend big items of equipment within your church.

Monthly

- Aim to cut your budget by 1 per cent and give it away.
- Buy Tearcraft gifts.
- Spend less on fashion items.
- Eat out less and give the money away.

Going deeper

- Promote Fairtrade Fortnight.
- Have a month (or Lent period) of living more simply.
- Try living on a cash basis for a month.
- Move part of your savings to Shared Interest.
- Campaign for trade justice.
- Don't replace your kitchen, bathroom or whatever but give the money away instead.

Useful websites

- **www.fairtrade.org.uk**   The Fairtrade Foundation's site highlights developments in the world of Fairtrade. They are sponsors of the annual Fairtrade Fortnight. The site highlights the availability of Fairtrade products, from roses to footballs, and where you can get them, as well as promoting Fairtrade Fortnight. I was upset when my order for an inflatable Fairtrade banana was delayed due to heavy demand, but it reached me eventually!

- **www.triodos.co.uk** Triodos bank was foun
  the Netherlands in 1980 and is one of Europe's larges
  ethical banks. It specializes in ethical banking and
  investment in small-scale enterprises in developing
  countries.
- **www.cafod.org.uk** CAFOD is the relief and development agency of the Catholic churches in England and
  Wales. It works in over sixty countries and has a
  strong emphasis on rights and values, drawing from
  its Christian roots. It has recently had a strong
  emphasis on living simply.
- **www.thesimpleway.org** The website of the Simple
  Way is a great place for accessing thinking on living
  in community, service as a lifestyle and taking community action. It is the home website of Shane
  Claiborne, author of *The Irresistible Revolution*.

CHAPTER 15

Action 8: Living Sustainably

Seas are filled both by mighty rivers and by drops of rain.
James Jones, Bishop of Liverpool, November 2006

Climate change is the greatest long-term challenge facing our planet. It threatens the very survival of humanity, and is already causing severe damage to the livelihoods of poor people in many countries. Climate change is the most extreme example of a wide range of human-induced damage to the environment, which includes pollution and deforestation. By 2050 there could be as many as 150 million environmental refugees.

Bishop James Jones spoke at the Stop Climate Chaos rally in London at the end of 2006, arguing that we need to work together to save the planet, and that both big and small contributions are vital. The drops of rain comprise the actions that we take as individuals to use our own resources more sustainably. The mighty rivers are the actions that governments and private companies need to take if global warming and other major environmental crises are to be addressed. The two are strongly linked. It is only as we practise living sustainably in our own lives that we will develop the passion and have the credibility to be able to campaign for the changes that are needed at national and international level.

The church, with some honourable exceptions, has been slow to prioritize environmental concern. Theologically we remain divided, and some still argue that environmental catastrophe is either inevitable or, indeed, to be welcomed as a sign of the end of the world and Christ's return. But there are also signs that churches are changing and doing a lot more. James Jones has written a book called *Jesus and the Earth* which explores Jesus' relationship to and teaching on the environment. He took a day out to go through this teaching with a group of Tearfund staff. He highlighted Jesus as creator and saviour of the universe and not just of people. He says: 'to desecrate the earth is not just a crime against the earth and future generations, which it is. To desecrate the earth is a blasphemy. It is to defile Christ's own gifts.'

What the Bible teaches

1. We are responsible for God's creation and accountable to him

> *The Lord God took the man and put him in the Garden of Eden to work it and take care of it.*   Genesis 2:15

This is God's world (Psalm 24:1). Creation was undertaken through and for Jesus (Colossians 1:20). God appoints us as stewards for creation and will hold us to account. We are to use the land and other resources sustainably (Leviticus 25:1–7).

2. We are interconnected and our actions have future consequences

> *God cannot be mocked. People reap what they sow.*
> Galatians 6:7

We must understand and take responsibility for the consequences of our actions. What we do will affect others and we must be concerned about their interests (Romans 13:9–10). We must care for poor people who are affected and help them to prepare and adapt. God will redeem the world (Romans 8:20–21).

3. We must not be selfish if others are suffering

> *...value others above yourselves, not looking to your own*
> *interests, but...to the interests of the others.*
>
> Philippians 2:3–4

It is not acceptable for us to indulge while others suffer. God keeps his greatest condemnation for those who enjoy their riches at the expense of poor people (James 5:1–5). That is what we are doing through environmental degradation. God himself will defend the needy and crush the oppressor (Psalm 72:4).

The urgency of environmental action

The evidence outlined in chapter 3 and elsewhere suggests that we are heading for climatic catastrophe. Ten years ago a book like this might not have had a chapter on your environmental impact, but it should have done. The signs of environmental damage have been there for decades and were recognized at the Rio Earth Summit in 1992. The shocking science of climate change and its implications for poor people around the world have dramatically raised the profile of environmental issues. But the UN Millennium Ecosystem report noted that two thirds of the ecosystems on which we depend are already currently being degraded or used unsustainably.[15.1] We now realize that our unsustainable use of the planet threatens to reverse the benefits of poverty reduction, leading to loss of homes and misery for millions of people. It is a crisis that sets the needs of poor people against the consumption and political priorities of the rich.

Climate change is likely to mean an increased severity of weather events including hurricanes, flooding and drought. Rich countries generate most greenhouse gases, but it is primarily poor people who will suffer. The review of the economics of climate change undertaken by Sir Nicholas Stern in 2006[15.2] suggested that it would be possible to maintain economic growth while addressing the causes of global warming at a cost of around 1 per cent of national income. He concluded then that we had ten years to take action. Despite some positive moves, however, politicians are not as yet taking action that is radical enough, and as each year goes past, the damage done, and the risks of irreversible change, continue to rise.

Climate change becomes real for me as I speak to Tearfund partners in various parts of the world. I went to Burkina Faso and saw the way in which the desert is moving south, and the seasons are becoming less reliable. In Ethiopia, malaria is becoming prevalent at higher altitudes, exposing new communities to the threat of this and other diseases. The snows of Kilimanjaro have all but disappeared. The melting of glaciers and changes in rainfall patterns worldwide threaten water supply to hundreds of millions of people.

The impact of drought in the Sahel

In Burkina Faso I met a man who had lost all forty of his animals in the recent drought. He was grateful for the food relief that had been provided, but his question was a simple one: 'How am I going to get back to where I was before?' Without animals his only option was to look for casual labour. But he was doing so at the same time as a host of other farmers who had also lost their livelihoods, and there was little work to be found. What he needed was intervention from outside to restore his capital, either through a gift or a loan, to allow him to get back to using his skills in a productive way.

What we have seen so far is likely to be dwarfed by the severity of future climate-related events. The science of climate change and its implications are frightening. Scientists project that the carbon dioxide emissions that have already been made will be enough to warm the planet by between 1.4 and 5.8 degrees during this century. The effects at the poles will be more severe, leading to a potentially catastrophic melting of ice. The loss of the Greenland ice cap could ultimately lead to a sea-level rise of around seven metres. This may take hundreds of years, but in the meantime accelerated sea-level rise will flood low-lying areas including huge parts of Bangladesh and several small island states.

What impact are you having?

Living simply is a good start towards limiting the damage that you do to the environment, but more is needed. Here are four key questions:

- Are you seeking to limit your carbon emissions?
- Do you recycle all that you can?
- Have you made a pledge about future air travel?
- Are you campaigning to stop climate chaos?

The answers to these questions involve the way in which you travel to work or school. Using a bicycle radically reduces the environmental impact of your travel, and, failing that, it is better to go by train or bus than by plane or car. Changing your energy supplier to one providing clean energy affects the amount of renewable energy being generated for the national grid.

To find out what impact you are having, go to www.carbonfootprint.com to estimate your own carbon emissions. You can then develop a personal carbon budget. Using the ideas from this chapter, you should be in a position to make some decisions about how you can reduce your emissions. Why not set a target of, say, 5 per cent reduction per year for the next five years?

Campaigners argue that most rich countries and consumers underestimate their carbon impact, because of the emissions produced in developing countries such as China to manufacture the goods that they consume.

A big dilemma

There is a huge dilemma for a book such as this related to climate change and air travel. My own and many other jobs depend on the ability to travel by air. On the one hand I urge you to travel and make contact with developing countries; on the other hand we know that this air travel will damage the environment.

I believe that the fundamental solution to the air travel issue is for governments to tax air travel so that prices rise and demand is reduced to a sustainable level. Air travel is a tremendous blessing to us all, and is not going to stop altogether. Although growing rapidly, it is not the primary source of carbon emissions, and we need an integrated approach, at both personal and national levels, to controlling our overall carbon budgets. Within that there will be some space for air travel, although not as much as we might want. What we need to do is to limit and prioritize our travel. We need to set a high threshold to justify flights, and to look for alternatives, such as greater use of videoconferencing in the business context. The carbon pledge site www.flightpedge.org.uk particularly challenges short-haul leisure flights. We need to ask two questions:

- In the context of living simply, is your proposed flight a good use of resources, both financial and environmental; and
- Do you have any other choices for transport, such as rail within the UK and Europe?

Ethical issues and the Christian response

Late one night I watched a television debate between an environmental activist (from the group 'Plane Stupid') and a representative of the air industry. The activist, a young man, spoke passionately about the impact of air travel on the poorest countries on earth; while the air industry representative appealed to people's greed and desire to continue to travel. I saw a choice laid out for our generation between selfish consumption causing damage to poor people, and a costly call to give up some of our luxuries for the sake of others. Which side are you on?

Christians have been slow to pick up this agenda. One very positive initiative has been A Rocha. Peter and Miranda Harris pioneered a Christian field study centre, called Cruzinha, in southern Portugal. I remember going there in the early 1990s and being amazed by the warblers and thrushes that they were weighing, measuring, ringing and then releasing as part of their ornothological research. Some of the fattest migrants had stored up so much food for their long migratory journeys that they could barely take off. A Rocha has now expanded into a global Christian environmental movement and network. It has set up a subsidiary called Climate Stewards, which is promoting a climate offset scheme that allows you to compensate for the environmental damage caused by travel, through supporting reforestation and small-scale energy projects.

Does carbon offsetting make a difference?

Offsetting air travel is the practice of paying an amount to compensate for the damage that you have done to the environment by your flight, through the emission of greenhouse gases. There are various websites at which you can compute the amounts to be paid, which vary depending on the basis of calculation, but are generally in the range of 3 to 10 per cent of the price of the ticket. If the money is then invested in appropriate projects, it may lead to a reduction in carbon emissions by others (for example, through more fuel-efficient stoves) or the capturing of atmospheric carbon dioxide (for example, through tree planting). Paying the extra amount may also lead you to reduce your consumption of flights, but the problem with offsetting is that it does not directly address the issues of how you are going to reduce your flying. Given the proliferation of offsetting companies, it is worth investigating what they intend to do with their money. Another option is simply to donate the equivalent amount to an organization investing in adaptation or campaigning about climate change. If this is a charity, then they can also reclaim tax on your donation.

Changing people's behaviour and government policy o issues provides an opportunity for leadership from the and individual Christians. Your carbon emissions make a difference. If individuals start to change, then there is a chance of generating a movement that will change policy. Sir John Houghton, a scientist, a Christian and the former co-chair of the Scientific Assessment Working Group of the Intergovernmental Panel on Climate Change, has proposed a scheme which will encourage Christians to reduce their carbon emissions and compensate for their overall carbon footprint (not just their air travel). The mechanism is called 'carbon sharing', and involves calculating your carbon emissions and then making a voluntary payment linked to the gap between your emissions and a sustainable global average. Such funds will then be used to help poorer countries to adapt to climate change, to develop sustainable energy and to improve their energy efficiency. It is hoped that this will provide a prototype for wider schemes to address these issues. The moral authority of the church backed by millions of committed and campaigning Christians is a formidable force. (See www.tearfund.org for more details.)

Sir John Houghton's contribution to the scientific debate on climate change has been significant. He has also worked to awaken the Christian church to these issues and to speak to the scientific and political worlds from a Christian perspective. He believes that the gospel has a key role in combating the selfishness and greed that have driven climate change and has played an important role in helping to change the opinions of church leaders in the US, which in turn has had an influence on US government policy

Reducing your emissions and developing a personal carbon budget

Sometimes it feels as though, if you can't be perfect, you might as well continue as you are. These are not all-or-nothing issues.

Any actions that you can take, however small, can make a difference. There are four main areas in which I recommend you should take action to reduce carbon emissions:

- Reducing your energy use at home and switching to a green electricity supplier.
- Recycling and reducing your consumption of energy-intensive products.
- Making your transport more environmentally friendly.
- Campaigning for changes in government policies.

Should we be buying locally produced goods?

Given the carbon implications of moving goods around the world, there is an argument for buying goods that are locally produced and require less transport. There are two problems with this. Firstly, it would prevent poorer countries from developing and taking advantage of trade, and secondly it ignores the emissions involved in the local production and distribution process, which can be as significant than those involved in long-haul travel, especially by sea. What we need is a comprehensive carbon labelling scheme which would allow us to avoid commodities with high carbon emissions in either their production or distribution.

Reducing your energy use

Each home in the UK produces about six tonnes of carbon dioxide each year; which is over a quarter of the nation's total emissions. The action required is simple: energy-efficient lighting, good insulation and efficient boilers and other machines. Switching to a green electricity provider increases the use of and investment in renewable energy. Tearfund recommends Good Energy (www.good-energy.co.uk).

There are a multitude of tips on how you can save energy on a day-to-day basis, such as:

- not over-filling your kettle;
- drawing curtains at night to retain heat;

- not leaving appliances on standby;
- turning down the temperature of your central heating;
- washing your clothes at lower temperatures; and
- always having a full load of washing.

See Tearfund's booklet *For Tomorrow Too* for more ideas.

Recycling

Over 70 per cent of our household rubbish could be recycled, but in the UK the actual figure is just 8 per cent. 80 per cent of our rubbish goes to landfill sites that then emit methane. You can compost your organic waste, and take a myriad of small actions that will make a difference. These include reusing plastic bags, or switching to longer-life bags made from sustainable materials; avoiding excess packaging (for example, on vegetables); stopping unwanted junk mail (register at www.mpsonline.org.uk); and reusing as much as you can, from envelopes to food containers and rechargeable batteries. Perhaps the easiest contribution you can make is just to consume less, especially of energy-intensive products. You can decide to make things last longer, and get them repaired rather then buying a replacement. All of these actions (as with the energy saving above) also save you money, which you can use to support poor communities.

Transport

Road transport is responsible for over a fifth of UK emissions. We need to share transport more, whether through public transport or car shares. We need to buy a fuel-efficient car and avoid short trips. My wife travels a lot by bicycle. One of my actions is to join her by buying a bike and reducing my car-related carbon emissions.

Air travel is the most rapidly growing contributor to global warming. The impact of your share of a single flight can be greater than several months of other transport. Air fares are so low because there is no global taxation system that forces you to pay the real cost of the damage that you are doing to the environment. You must fly less and urge governments to take the politically unpopular step of taxing flights so that travellers pay the true cost of the damage they are causing. You can opt to travel by train wherever possible within the UK and to the near abroad, especially France and Belgium. When you do fly, then offset. Wouldn't it also be encouraging if governments did more to make rail and bus travel less expensive?

Campaigning for change in national and international responses

Radical political action is needed within the next ten years to avoid the worst impacts of climate change. It will only happen, however, if there is massive, worldwide, public pressure for change. Otherwise, the rich countries seem likely to respond too slowly. This is because of the lags in the effect of carbon emissions on climate, the vested interests of major industries in the status quo and the politically unpopular nature of the action that is needed. The emerging economic superpowers, including China and India, will not easily be willing to sacrifice their own economic growth to reduce emissions. We therefore need to lobby governments. Stop Climate Chaos is a coalition of NGOs in the UK seeking to put pressure on governments to change, and has developed the 'I Count' campaign which you can join.

Climate change is a global problem that can only be tackled collectively. Governments need to have domestic emissions targets with annual milestones and commit themselves to reductions that go well beyond the existing Kyoto commitments. We need governments to rebalance taxation so that the full costs of energy use are captured, to encourage fuel-efficient technologies, to support energy saving and so on. Given the negative environmental impact of air travel, there is an overwhelming case for taxing airline fuel to reflect these costs.

A global target needs to be set to keep temperature rise below a level of two degrees above pre-industrial levels, which is the limit proposed by scientists if we are to avoid catastrophic climate change. If carbon reduction is not to become anti-development, then poor countries need to be allowed to expand their emissions within this overall framework. The churches in the UK, the US and beyond have a key role to hold governments to account and to lead a debate that focuses on these vital issues.

Helping people to reduce risks and adapt

Whatever we do in the next ten to twenty years, we know that carbon dioxide already emitted will cause massive changes to our global climate. This is already affecting the poorest communities on earth and will get worse. What should the development community be doing? Approaches to disaster risk reduction which help communities prepare and adapt will be vital. There are a host of measures that can make a difference, from the design and location of houses to the types of crops that are grown, the management of water resources and reforestation. Huge resources will be required beyond existing aid budgets to help farmers and others respond to changing climates. Research is needed to highlight the threats and to identify technologies that will help communities to respond.

Scientists suggest that the impact of climate change will be more extreme in vulnerable areas. We are already seeing this on the edges of major deserts and at the poles. This means that we need to focus assistance on these most vulnerable communities. Climate change is likely to lead to a greater intensity of extreme weather events, especially hurricanes. We know the countries which are most vulnerable, and should invest now to help communities be prepared. Tearfund is working with partners to develop a network of agencies in the most disaster-prone countries worldwide. They are able to respond when disaster strikes, and also work with communities now to help them prepare.

Adaptation to climate change

Climate change is already affecting poor communities, and increasing action will be needed to help people adapt to the changes it will bring. Jemed is a Tearfund partner that works with the Tuareg people in Niger to help preserve their nomadic lifestyles. As rains have become more erratic, Jemed has worked with the community to dig wells and build dykes to collect rainwater. It has also provided loans for buying animals, and education for the children; all of this helping the nomads to maintain their traditional culture in the face of climate change. The project also meets spiritual needs. The activities of Jemed are a practical testimony to the love of Christ. When severe drought affected the region in 2005, Jemed was able to use its network of relationships to deliver emergency support to needy families.

Taking action

Living sustainably requires a mixture of actions; some will cost us money and some will save it, but all help to move us towards a more sustainable future and act as a prophetic sign to the rest of the world. There are big one-off steps that involve your energy (such as switching electricity supplier) and transport (making a pledge about how often you will fly), but much of the action is about the myriad of small things that we can all do to save energy. Going deeper is to involve others and work together to reduce your collective energy use by equipment and car sharing, for example.

One-off actions

- Switch to a renewable energy supplier.
- Make energy savings in your home.
- Sign a flight pledge.

- Buy a bicycle.
- Sign up to the I Count campaign

Daily/weekly

- Recycle.
- Use your bicycle or public transport.
- Reuse your plastic bags at supermarkets.

Monthly

- Campaign for government action against excess packaging or other causes of waste and carbon emissions.
- Reduce your carbon emissions by 5 per cent per year.
- Offset carbon for your flights.
- Lower your thermostat.

Going deeper

- Eat less meat (vegetable protein is a more efficient use of resources).
- Find some ways to cut your cost of living by 10 per cent and give it away.
- Set up an equipment-sharing pool in your church.
- Contribute to the new carbon-sharing arrangement.

Internet resources and other contacts

- **www.arocha.org** A Rocha is the leading Christian conservation charity. Founded in Portugal, it has expanded to be a family of projects working in Europe, the Middle East, Africa, North and South America, Australia and Asia. A Rocha projects are frequently cross-cultural in character, and share a community emphasis, with a focus on science and research, practical conservation and environmental education. Climate Stewards has been set up by A Rocha to encourage people to reduce their carbon footprint and to offset their necessary carbon emissions (see http://www.climatestewards.net).

- **www.jri.org.uk** The John Ray Initiative is an educational charity focused on environmental issues. It seeks to bring together Christian and scientific perspectives. Its current major focus is on climate change and its website gives access to a range of papers, presentations, Bible studies and other resources related to creation care.
- **www.foe.co.uk** Friends of the Earth campaigns on a range of environmental issues and undertakes research to highlight ways in which we are damaging our environment and what we can do about them.
- **www.actonco2.direct.gov.uk** The Act On CO_2 site is a UK government site with excellent graphics and a calculator to find out your carbon footprint. It then has some tips for simple changes to help tackle climate change.

CHAPTER 16

Action 9: Giving

We have lived here since I was born, but I've found that life is changing. Some of the problems we were facing are being reduced. Now we are getting water from our own village. This is development for people in Uhambingeto.

Joyce Mbwilo, Tanzania

Joyce Mbwilo is a mother who lives in Uhambingeto, in rural Tanzania. She featured in Tearfund's campaign for Make Poverty History in 2005. She used to walk fourteen miles a day to collect water, before a Tearfund-supported project installed a safe and reliable water supply in her village. Her example inspired some young people at St Philip's Church in Girlington, Bradford, to share her experience by carrying water on their heads. Even in relay teams, it took them four hours to carry the water fourteen miles.

I met Joyce during my first Tearfund overseas visit in the second half of 2005. It seemed strange to meet someone who was so familiar from her photographs. We had a good time showing Joyce the shirts that had been produced for Make Poverty History with her face on the front. I sensed something of Joyce's warmth and joy. But the problems of Uhambingeto are far from solved. Although progress has been made on provision of water and health facilities, the area is still subject to frequent droughts, markets are difficult and expensive to access, and HIV and other diseases are a constant threat.

It is an immense privilege to be able to use money to change the world. Small sums saved in rich countries can make a huge difference in a poor environment if correctly channelled. The price of a chocolate bar or coffee can provide life-saving drugs. Money can't solve all of life's problems but it can solve some. It can be used to restore homes after the earthquake in Pakistan, to feed orphans in Zimbabwe or to finance church mobilization in Latin America.

There is a big debate within the church on how much to give to whom and whether we should tithe – that is, to give away 10 per cent of our income. Given the needs of the world, the simplest maxim is that of John Wesley: 'Earn what you can, save what you can, give what you can.' As Rick Warren says about tithing on the Saddleback Church website: 'If you don't want to be legalistic about this, then just give away 20 or 30%.' Let's commit ourselves to giving away more. The only money that lasts for eternity is the money that we give away.

What the Bible teaches

1. We are encouraged to give regularly, joyfully, sacrificially and without expecting any return

> *God loves a cheerful giver.*   2 Corinthians 9:7

The Bible says that all good things come from God (James 1:17). Money is to meet our needs, for giving away and to support community celebrations that involve poor people. The hoarding of wealth is condemned. Each person should give what they have decided in their heart. 2 Corinthians 8 and 9 provide a guide to being a good giver – generous, sacrificial and joyful.

2. The primary focus of New Testament giving is to meet the needs of poor people and Christian workers

> *...your plenty will supply what they need...*
>
>   2 Corinthians 8:14

New Testament giving is geared primarily towards poor people and not towards the church. The New Testament church gave sacrificially to poor people (Acts 2:44–45; 4:32–35; 6:1–2). We are called to focus on our responsibilities. There are no limits as to who is our neighbour. We must be generous both to other Christians and to those in need outside the church (Luke 10:29–37).

3. As we give, we will be blessed

Those who give to the poor will lack nothing.

Proverbs 28:27

There is a virtuous circle in which both giver and receiver are blessed and glory goes to God. Our giving results in blessings to us but not necessarily in the form of increased wealth (2 Corinthians 9:11–14). God has promised to supply all our needs in the context of giving (Philippians 4:19).

Giving as a way of life

You might expect a book by a Tearfund employee to be positive about giving. I am. But I am also very conscious of the limitations of giving. It is extremely difficult to give money away. Giving so easily destroys trust and gives the wrong incentives. The nature of relationships is distorted, there are dangers of corruption, of misunderstanding, of dependency and deception. History provides numerous examples of such relationships that have gone wrong. So why do we do it and how can we ensure that our gifts have a positive impact?

Ultimately we give because God tells us to, and gives us clear guidelines so that our giving can be effective. There is a huge amount that can be achieved though wise giving. Most charities could not function without the support of individuals. Giving money can save lives, reduce suffering and provide hope for the future. Giving and receiving are an adventure at the heart of our discipleship. There is a cycle through which we give, and then rely on God for our own needs. This is good news for the people who receive our gifts and good news for us as we see God provide. Both parties grow in faith, needs are met, and everyone praises God. You can start this cycle by giving. Generosity builds faith.

How we give is more difficult. Imagine that you are thinking about whether to give to a beggar. Part of you says, 'Just do it!' Another part says, 'What if he or she spends it on alcohol? Will I make things worse?' Many of us have worked this through and come to a solution, but it is important to recognize that in reducing poverty, as in our personal relationships, there are good and bad ways of giving. I was challenged to hear that Strømme Foundation, a Christian charity in Norway, requires its beneficiaries to raise 20 per cent of project costs, which increases local ownership of projects and reduces dependency.

The Cottage Café

In my kitchen I have a tea-towel from the remarkable Cottage Café in Torquay. For over twenty years this ministry of Upton Vale Baptist Church, staffed by volunteers, has channelled its profits into Christian development projects worldwide. The team has supported a kindergarten in Moldova over several years. It has given, amongst many others, £800 to help nomads in Tibet who had lost their yaks in a hard winter, £10,000 for a home for street children in Ukraine, and gifts for improved nutrition in Afghanistan and electricity provision in Kenya. Recent gifts have included support to AIDS orphans in Kenya and Uganda. All the tea, coffee and chocolate is, of course, Fairtrade. The café is currently recruiting new volunteers. So if you are looking for an opportunity to serve...

So how much should we give and to whom? The answer is to give as much as we can in faith and with a peaceful heart. God will always give back more than we have given, through increased joy and freedom, and, sometimes, through increased material wealth. Through giving, we can learn to escape from our obsession with things. You need to decide how much to get involved with the organizations you support. Some find that direct involvement gives meaning to their giving, while others are happy to stay at arm's length and trust the charity to use the money wisely.

Giving regularly and occasionally, giving dramatically

God calls on us to give regularly. We give to support our local church and to meet the needs of poor people. Some people give to their church which in turn gives away a proportion of its income. It makes sense as a taxpayer to give tax efficiently, and take advantage of any tax reclaim that you can make from your government to benefit the charity concerned. The best plan is to set up regular direct debits for giving, so that organizations have a reliable income and you can claim back income tax with minimum effort, for example through the Gift Aid scheme in the UK. But don't let that inhibit spontaneous generosity too. Having developed your action plan, you may want to give to organizations that are involved in the issues and countries that you have prioritized.

How much should you give? The most important principle is that this is between you and God. There are many books about the benefits of tithing, or giving 10 per cent of your income away. Some people give all of this to the church and others split it between their church and mission or development agencies. From time to time you can look at options to give away more. It is important to consider how much you live on as well as how much you give away. It is not fair for people on higher wages to give the same proportion. What about moving to the graduated tithe, as recommended by Ron Sider and outlined below?

The graduated tithe

The graduated tithe involves giving away an increasing proportion of your income as that income rises. One model is to tithe your income up to the average wage in your country and then give an increasing proportion thereafter. In the UK, for example, that might involve tithing up to £25,000 (about the current full-time average wage) and then giving away, say, 20 per cent of the next £10,000, 30 per cent of the following £10,000 up to a maximum of 50 per cent for income above £55,000 per year.

There are also times in your life for more dramatic one-off giving. It is a wonderful feeling to give away a wad of banknotes in response to God's call. It is good to keep an ear open to God about times when he might want you to give sacrificially. There is much to learn from the American tradition of philanthropy. Whatever your views of a system that allows individuals to accumulate such wealth, it is inspiring to see first Bill Gates and then Warren Buffett give away over $30 billion each to the Gates Foundation for charitable uses. Some benefactors seek to immortalize themselves through plaques and the naming of buildings, or even park benches. God calls on us to give with no thought of ourselves and a reward only in heaven. It gives him pleasure and honour when we choose to do so.

Our wealth and opportunities to give vary considerably over our life-cycle. When income is low it is good to think about how you can give through alternative gift catalogues (such as 'Living Gifts', see www.livinggifts.org.uk), charity credit cards and one-off gifts. For many of us there may also be one or two occasions when we have resources to spare and a specific opportunity to give in a more dramatic way. This might be when we receive an inheritance, when we get a lump sum on retirement or when we sell a house. We may only be able to do this when we die, and it is vitally important to make a will to ensure that we use our resources as God leads us. One of the advantages of giving a spectacular gift before we die is that we can have some involvement in where it goes and the impact that it has. Many charities have schemes for large-scale donors that allow you to see and maintain links with the specific project that you have funded. What a privilege!

The once-in-a-lifetime project

It is good to get excited about planning for a once-in-a-lifetime gift. Possibly when you retire and get a lump sum, or inherit some money, you could give away a substantial sum. What could you do? Perhaps you have seen some specific needs during your lifetime or met some great people whom you could trust with a lump sum. Perhaps you could set up a bursary in one of your focus countries, or with one of the organizations you are supporting, to finance some work into the future. I pray that God will give you an opportunity and a great idea.

There are several organizations that can help you with the mechanics of giving and ensure that you maximize your tax benefits. The one that I have had most contact with is called Stewardship. They offer a range of services to allow one-off and regular giving to be tax efficient. See www.stewardship.org.uk.

What to give to?

It makes sense to use your giving to reinforce and support your priorities both in terms of countries and areas of work. It is good to support the full range of integral mission work, including evangelism and development. There are very few organizations that are not looking for money, so how do you assess a good organization? Especially if you are going to give over an extended period, it is worth investing some time to check out the organization concerned. It is right to want to ensure that the money has the maximum impact and is not subject to fraud or waste. Here is a checklist:

- Are the vision and objectives of the organization linked to your priorities?
- Is it registered as a charity and subject to regulation?
- Are there published financial accounts which you can read?
- What are the percentage fund-raising and administration costs?
- What is the sectoral and geographical focus of the organization?
- Does it seek to serve the poorest or influence those who have power to bring change?
- Is it committed to integral mission?
- What is the philosophy and basis of faith of the organization?
- Does it seek to build the church?

The new Standard Information Return required by the UK Charity Commissioners will help you decide. Find them at www.charitycommission.gov.uk. Be warned, however, that it is often hard to disentangle administration costs, particularly for work such as advocacy that requires staff in the head office.

As well as choosing the countries and sectors that you want to support, it makes sense to look at what others are doing. Some charities get high levels of income and are often in the public eye. Others, perhaps equally deserving, get very little. Certain countries (for example, Francophone Africa in the UK), activities and types of disaster are often neglected. You can increase the impact of your giving by focusing on relatively neglected countries and organizations.

Responding to disasters

Giving needs to be spontaneous as well as planned. Our response to the urgent needs of others says much about our hearts. But when you see a disaster, how much should you give and to whom? How can you assess the needs? Any charity is free to appeal to its supporters and the general public for any emergency. There is a system in the UK, however, where major charities work together through the Disasters Emergency Committee (DEC) in the context of major disasters to launch a joint appeal.

God and the tsunami

Major disasters often provoke theological debate. Out of the tsunami has come one of the most thoughtful reflections I have ever read on God and suffering, from Ajith Fernando, the national director for Youth for Christ in Sri Lanka. In *After the Tsunami* he highlights the need to mourn and lament, and to cry out to God with our hard questions. From such grief comes an opportunity to trust in God's sovereignty, and a motivation for action.

Ajith argues that both groaning and worship are essential for those responding to disaster. God also groans, and Jesus knows what it is to experience suffering both in his life and death. Disasters are a warning to us of the eternal realities of death and judgment. They are a wake-up call to the church and to the world. Disasters provide an opportunity to demonstrate God's love and grace through self-sacrifice and service. They are a time for prayer and for giving, both locally and internationally, and for providing God's comfort. Christian agencies must work in disasters in a godly way and avoid fraud and other abuses.

We must also work to prevent disaster. By investing in disaster risk reduction we can help reduce the impact of disasters in the future. Through education, better preparedness and investment in emergency facilities, communities can be better prepared when disaster strikes. Suffering avoided will never hit the headlines, but is vital to protect vulnerable people.

There are thirteen agencies in the DEC, including the Red Cross, Oxfam and Christian Aid. For more details see their website at www.dec.org. Agencies receive various shares of the appeal money. Tearfund's share is about 5 per cent. You can choose either to give to the DEC, or directly to the charity of your choice. For the 2004 tsunami appeal, Tearfund received £10 million directly from supporters and £19 million as our 5 per cent share of the DEC appeal, which received an unprecedented level of donations.

The bias in giving is perhaps more extreme in emergencies than in any other area. Crises that have high media coverage, such as the tsunami, tend to receive large responses. Others are neglected. It makes sense for governments to support non-specific humanitarian funds which allow more rapid responses and provide resources for under-funded disasters. It is also helpful to give the organizations you support some leeway, by not specifying too closely what needs to be done with the money. All organizations need support for their running costs which, if reasonable, are legitimate. There are also occasions where disasters are over-funded and where allowing funds to be transferred to an area of greater need can have an increased impact.

Some common questions

Is child sponsorship a good idea?

One specific question often raised is whether child sponsorship is a good idea for giving. Is it an expensive marketing gimmick in which children are selected for special treatment? Or a fund-raising tool for community development in which the benefits to the individual are minimal? Or is it a powerful and direct personal link that benefits both the individual child and the community in which he or she lives? The idea of child sponsorship involves a long-term commitment to community development and at its best can be part of an effective development approach. But the relationship aspects come at a cost.

Most sponsorship schemes do not give excessive specific benefits to individuals, but are based around projects for whole communities. The individual children are beneficiaries and are then asked to form a direct relationship with one specific donor to provide real feedback. Extras are limited to the presents sent by donors and occasional schemes for all the sponsored children or the community as a whole. The drawback is the extra overhead costs that forming a relationship incurs. Costs are required for administration, for arranging the exchange of correspondence and for providing customized information to the sponsor. The positive side is the relationship that is created, which can make giving come alive and promotes prayer and personal engagement. The funding tends to be reliable and long term, thus providing security and sustainable benefits to communities. There is no doubt that community development objectives can be achieved with lower administration costs by traditional projects and I would encourage you to give through such routes. But the judgment as to whether the increased ownership, commitment and prayer that result from child sponsorship are worth the additional costs needs to be made by each individual donor, preferably on the basis of clear cost information.

Should I support alternative gift catalogues?

Alternative gift catalogues are a great way to challenge our consumerist society, especially at Christmas, and to give gifts that are linked to the needs of poor people. It is also helpful to have an indication of what impact your money will have. Many charities will say that a gift of £10 can provide a certain amount of food for a family or some specific healthcare item. Those who produce catalogues, however, need to be explicit about the extent to which resources given will actually go to the intended items, such as buying a goat, or to more general funds. Read the small print to see if you are really buying a specific item, or making a more general contribution to a programme in which such items are provided. You can then decide whether you are happy with what is on offer. Catalogues have been a very effective means of fundraising for many organizations over the past few years. Since money in an organization can be moved around, however, it is important that you feel happy with the overall policies and spending of an organization as well as the specific item that you are purchasing.

Does my money go to poor people or does it get spent on administration?

All charities require administrative costs to run their own organizations. These should be presented as transparently as possible. The Charity Commissioners in the UK are seeking to improve financial reporting by charities so that these figures can be seen and compared amongst organizations. You should look to ensure that as high a proportion of your gift as possible reaches poor communities. In considering overheads, however, it is also important to think about the quality and effectiveness of the spending. If a charity is spending money on good project design and monitoring, then this is likely to be money well spent, and preferable to an organization that passes out grants in poor countries with little accountability.

Can my money make any difference – won't the problems be the same next year?

Both charities and the people giving to them are increasingly focused on the impact of their support. The needs of developing countries are acute and there will not be a quick resolution to many deep-seated problems. But it is possible to see improvements in the economic, health and education status of communities over time. Tearfund's interventions in the food crisis in Southern Africa in 2005 found that communities that had been helped in the previous crisis in 2002 were more resilient and able to cope with the new crisis.

Doesn't aid all get swallowed up by corruption?

Perhaps the commonest response of those who are sceptical about the value of development assistance is that it will all pass into the hands of corrupt governments and officials. There is no doubt that the most corrupt countries in the world are also amongst the poorest. Major government and private-sector contracts are at risk from corrupt practices. But most development agencies go to great lengths to ensure that funds are well used, in part to safeguard their own reputations which are vital to future sustainability. For example, by working through the church and Christian organizations, Tearfund seeks to minimize the risk of corruption. But there will always be some losses. This is a necessary price if one is to take risks in working in difficult situations to meet the needs of the poorest. The challenge for all charities is to ensure that these losses are minimized.

Corruption matters because it is wrong and damaging. It increases the cost of operating in an economy and reduces the prospects for investment. It cheats consumers of their rights and often, particularly in the case of corrupt building contracts, endangers their safety. The international group Transparency International has played a central role in highlighting corruption, including through its annual league table (see www.transparency.org). Transparency International is worthy of support as it battles in often dangerous situations to highlight and reduce corruption.

It takes two parties for there to be a bribe. We should campaign to ensure that Western companies act ethically and do not pay bribes. Initiatives such as the Extractive Industries Transparency Initiative (see www.eitransparency.org) are encouraging countries and companies to be more open about the payments that are made and received for major mineral resources, especially oil. We can ask difficult questions as shareholders. We can encourage and support investigative journalism. The church itself needs to stand against ingrained corruption, which requires courage.

Taking action

How about setting a target for the amount that you would like to give away over the next year? Make it a stretching one. Seek God for what you should give to, and the impact that you want to see that money have. Pray in the income to make it happen. Consider organizing a fund-raising event to involve your friends or going on a sponsored challenge of some sort.

The great thing about giving is that once decisions are made on your regular monthly commitments, you can continue to have wide-ranging and long-lasting impact with minimal further action. You can also use your will to leave hope for poorer people after your death. More people now are giving occasional lump sums, which you can link to an annual review of your financial position. More radically, you could move towards giving on the basis of a graduated tithe, which increases as your income rises, and look for opportunities to fund a major project as your circumstances allow.

One-off actions

- Make a will.
- Review and increase your giving.

Daily/weekly

- Move to a graduated tithe.
- Have a jar to collect loose change and savings.

Monthly

- Set up standing orders.

Going deeper

- Consider a major giving project.
- Undertake an annual review of your assets – give away a high proportion of any bonus you get.
- Encourage your church to give more towards poverty reduction.
- Sell some of your goods on eBay and give the money away.
- Send some valuables to be auctioned for charity (for example, by Northwood Missionary Auctions at www.nmauctions.org.uk).

Internet resources and other contacts

- **www.stewardship.org.uk**   Stewardship is a Christian organization dedicated to helping with the planning and administration of charitable giving.
- **www.livinggenerously.com**   Living Generously is a site sponsored by the 24-7 movement that allows you to channel gifts that you both give and receive to projects around the world that will meet the needs of poor people.
- **www.tearfund.org/giving**   Tearfund relies primarily on the gifts of individual supporters to fund its work through partners worldwide. Tearfund also manages teams directly responding to major disasters and political emergencies in some of the toughest environments in the world including Darfur, Afghanistan and the Democratic Republic of Congo.
- The two major Christian child sponsorship organizations in the UK are World Vision (www.worldvision.org.uk), which is the largest Christian development organization worldwide, and Compassion International (www.compassion.com). In addition to its development programmes, World

Vision UK undertakes a wide range of advocacy and development education work. Compassion is strongly focused on children and child advocacy issues.

- There are a range of smaller UK-based Christian development charities including CORD, (www.cord.org.uk), which specializes in post-conflict work, and Send A Cow (www.sendacow.org.uk), which has genuine expertise in supplying livestock and the associated training and advice to some of Africa's most vulnerable groups.

PART 4

Taking It Forward

CHAPTER 17

Implementing Your Own Action Plan

Far too often, governments and commentators simply wring their hands in despair at the problem rather than taking the simple practical steps that will bring about long term, powerful, permanent change.

Dr Kiran Martin, 2005 Rendle Short Lecture

In 2006 I travelled with Elaine Storkey, the International President of Tearfund, to visit Kiran Martin at the Asha Project in Delhi. Women and girls from the slum led us in worship and then dancing in a small room. We saw a church that had been planted in a slum, employment created, love shown and lives transformed. I brought home a beautiful scarf that I had bought as a present for my mother, and wondered at how something so exquisite could emerge from such squalid conditions. This is the story of Asha; a picture of integral mission in action.

Kiran Martin started her medical work in the Delhi slums with a stethoscope and a desk under a tree in 1988. Today, her model of transformation is recognized globally. Over 200,000 slum dwellers have had their lives touched by Asha's work and there have been dramatic improvements in maternal and child mortality and the incidence of major diseases. Women volunteers from the communities have been empowered and have taken responsibility, both for themselves, and for the groups they serve.

All of this has flowed from one woman's vision of using her skills in God's strength to serve women in Delhi's slums, one of the poorest and most powerless groups in the world. From humble beginnings, she has created a unique partnership between Asha, the Government and the slum dwellers that has been widely imitated. It is a powerful demonstration of what a single life can achieve. As well as service provision, Kiran has engaged in a range of advocacy issues related to the rights of families living in the slums. She has persistently campaigned for women slum dwellers to be able to get title for their land, which would give them both security and potentially collateral for borrowing to finance their own businesses. For more details of Asha's work go to www.asha-india.org.

What the Bible teaches

1. The way you live matters

> *If you can find but one person who deals honestly and seeks the truth, I will forgive this city.*   Jeremiah 5:1

God watches over your life and wants you to imitate him and be holy. If you invest your life for poor people, then God promises his guidance and blessing (Isaiah 58:10–12). If you are willing to die to self and serve others, then you can see the impact of your life multiplied (John 12:24). God gives us talents and expects us to use them and not bury them. It is not enough to be moved by poverty; we need to do something about it. Faith without action is dead (James 2:17).

2. You can have an impact

> *Always give yourselves fully to the work of the Lord, because you know that your labour in the Lord is not in vain.*   1 Corinthians 15:58

God has great plans for our lives and wants us to achieve things of eternal value. There will be a cost, and we are to be living sacrifices (Romans 12:1). But there is also great reward. We will see Jesus in the face of those we serve. As we go in faith, God will do much more than we could ever imagine (Ephesians 3:20). Our efforts, when inspired by God, will have an impact, whether or not we see it. It is worth making a sacrifice, both for the benefit of poor people and to please God. As we listen to and obey his prompting, we will see lasting fruit in our lives (John 15; 1 Corinthians 3).

3. We can get a better return by investing in heaven through serving poor people

> *Do not store up for yourselves treasures on earth ... store up for yourselves treasures in heaven.*   Matthew 6:19–20

One day we will see him face to face to hear his 'well done' (Matthew 25:21) and be welcomed into heaven by those whose lives we have impacted. Jesus encourages us to lay up treasure in heaven (Matthew 6:20). We may not know many people here and now, but we can bless people through our prayers and giving. In eternity, how many people from the great crowd from every nation on earth will want to thank you for what your sacrifice has achieved? (Revelation 7:9).

Finalizing the action plan

Kiran Martin challenges us all to take the simple, practical steps that will bring long-term change and free people from poverty. I hope that you are now both prepared and inspired to turn ideas into action, and to sustain and increase the work that you have already started. In chapter 7 you developed a priority and prayer list that highlighted key countries, people, issues and organizations on which you want to focus, and a draft action plan. I pray that God also gave you a vision and some goals. Chapters 8 to 16 should have given you a range of practical ideas as to how you can take this forward.

The final step is to review your original action plan and do a revised version, using the template at Annex 2, or from www.tearfund.org/poornomore. Pray and seek God's confirmation for the direction in which you are heading. As you do so, you might also want to go back to chapter 7 and see whether your new plan addresses the key areas where you wanted to increase your response. Look again at the actions proposed at the end of each of chapters 8 to 16 and see if there are any more that you want to add to your list.

It is important to stress that these steps are only tools and that it is the journey that counts. If you have not found the action plan approach to be a helpful one for you, I hope that you will still have picked up some ideas that you can implement.

Embedding actions into your life

If you are feeling excited, enthusiastic and eager to get on and do something, then great! Make the most of it and do some things immediately that will make a lasting difference. Set aside a couple of hours and consider whether you can do any of the one-off actions listed at the ends of the chapters, which can be linked to your priorities and will have a long-lasting impact. Some examples might include:

- Contact a solicitor and make a will.
- Set up one or more standing orders.
- Change your electricity supplier or bank account.
- Subscribe to the magazines of your priority agencies.
- Shift some of your savings to Shared Interest or a similar scheme.
- Start a scrapbook and an electronic file for press cuttings, photos etc.
- Revise your travel arrangements to be more energy efficient.

To make lasting change, you have to integrate your new pattern of action into your life. The effectiveness of our lives is in part determined by the habits that we develop. That is why the schedule suggests committing yourself to regular activities on a daily and weekly basis, with a session once a month to review progress. In doing so I suggest that you also keep a diary to record prayer requests and action taken and to mark progress towards your objectives and vision.

If you are finding that God is challenging you deeply on these issues, then you might want to go further. Spend time in prayer and fasting and see if God is leading you to work in a specific country or with a specific people group, which may call for language learning and a change of life. If you are considering volunteering, then go to the country on holiday to get a flavour. You may also want to consider a one-off project involving a substantial proportion of your wealth.

Encouraging others

Part of the action plan involves thinking about who we can work with and inspire in order to multiply our own efforts. If you have found the book helpful, then encourage some of your friends and family to go through it and adopt the same approach. Talk to those closest to you about your vision and see if there any projects that you can take forward together. Take some action at your church. Pray for your leaders. Build on the international contacts that the church already has and consider including them in your own priority list.

Your plan within God's plan

Your vision will be a small part of God's overall vision for the world. It is good to spend time reflecting on God's plan and purpose and to locate your vision firmly within his broader plan. We can be confident that God wants good things for his world now, when we consider what he has planned for the renewed earth in eternity. It seems fitting in this final chapter to reflect on the magnificent vision of the last two chapters of the Bible, Revelation 21 and 22.

- The first heaven and earth will pass away and with them all the poverty and suffering of this life.
- The dwelling of God will be with us.
- He will wipe away every tear.
- There will be no more death or mourning or crying or pain.
- God will make everything new.
- He will be the light.
- The thirsty will drink without cost.
- Those who overcome will inherit the new kingdom.
- The leaves of the trees by the river of life will be for the healing of the nations.
- No longer will there be any curse.
- God's people, including those who have been poor and oppressed, will reign with him for ever and ever.

All of us will one day see Jesus face to face. One of the biggest factors that will determine the impact of your life is whether you have put into practice your good intentions in relation to freeing people from poverty. Let's work for his 'well done'.

Keeping going

2007 marked the 200th anniversary of the abolition of the slave trade in the British Empire. It was achieved in part through the efforts of William Wilberforce and a group of Christian friends who campaigned tirelessly for over twenty years, with Wilberforce repeatedly bringing bills for abolition before Parliament. They then carried on for another twenty-six years until slavery itself became illegal.

Relationships and change both take time. If you persist, God has promised that you will see fruit eventually. As your life develops you will see God bringing together experiences and people from different situations to achieve something special. Be encouraged; God is at work in you to achieve all that he has prepared in advance for you to accomplish for him.

What legacy will you leave?

How will you know what you have achieved? There is a tension between wanting to focus on outcomes and the sense from the Bible that we must leave them in God's hands. Results are not necessarily the reward of faithfulness. The key is being courageous and obedient in what God is calling you to do and giving all the glory to him. I believe that much of our impact will only be revealed in eternity, but there are things that we can see God doing here and now. Keeping a record of prayers prayed and answered, churches growing, government policies changing, prisoners released, can be a tremendous encouragement. God calls you to be faithful. Sometimes you will see the outcomes of your work, and sometimes you won't.

Some of the measures proposed sound small, but think about the impact you can achieve if you carry them on consistently. A plan to give £50 per month would add up to £18,000 over 30 years and the chance to affect literally hundreds of lives. A letter once a month over the same period means that you will have campaigned on behalf of 360 people. This illustrates the accumulated results of positive habits.

So what will be the story of the rest of your life? You may feel that you could have done more in the past. But be encouraged. It is never too late. The key question is how you are going to take this forward from now. My prayer is that you will commit yourself to take action, institute good habits and then go out and make a difference. And in doing so, you will also inspire your friends and family to change the world.

What legacy will you leave? As well as the kind things that people will say at your funeral about your character, wouldn't it be great to discover in eternity that your life had made a tangible difference for many people in the poorest countries of the world. There is no reason why there should not be thousands of people in heaven who have benefited from the choices that you have made – people who became *poor no more* because you helped to spread the gospel and reduce poverty. What a party to look forward to!

I have put into this book many of the ideas that I have gathered in my career and personal life, but it would be great if you were to push out in faith and go way beyond my vision. My prayer is for God to build a movement of Christians committed to these goals, living the adventure together. I would love to hear if, for example, you have decided to learn Amharic and make contact with the local Ethiopian community, or to take any other radical action. You can write to me at:

> Peter Grant
> Tearfund
> 100 Church Road
> Teddington
> Middlesex
> TW11 8QE
> UK
> (email: peter.grant@tearfund.org)

Your biggest legacy will be in terms of the difference that you have made to other people. If during your life you inspire ten people to get more engaged in caring about poverty and justice issues, then just think about the potential impact of that over time. And may all the glory go to God (Psalm 115:1)!

So lay up your treasures in heaven and, while I think of it, have you made a will yet?

A Priority and Prayer List

	Prayer day	Prayer targets
Countries		
	Monday	
	Tuesday	
	Wednesday	
	Thursday	
Organizations		
	Friday	
	Saturday	
	Sunday	
People		
	Monday	
	Tuesday	
	Wednesday	
Issues		
	Thursday	
	Friday	
	Saturday	
	Sunday	
Vision: *What am I looking to see God do?*		

An Action Plan

Date				
Sources of information				
Global action	One-off/ annual	Daily/weekly	Monthly action day	Going deeper
Praying				
Campaigning				
Serving				
Making friends				
Involving others				
Mobilizing your church				
Living simply				
Living sustainably				
Giving				
Ideas for local action				
Other ideas to follow up				

Bibliography

Tokunboh Adeyemo (ed.), *African Bible Commentary*, Zondervan, 2006

Peter Bauer, *Dissent on Development*, Weidenfeld and Nicolson, 1976

R. J. Berry (ed.), *When Enough is Enough*, Apollos, 2007

Phil Bowyer, *A Different World*, Authentic Lifestyle, 2005

Robert Chambers, *Whose Reality Counts? Putting the First Last*, Intermediate Technology, 1997

Tim Chester (ed.), *Justice, Mercy and Humility: Integral Mission and the Poor*, Paternoster, 2002

Tim Chester, *Good News to the Poor*, IVP, 2004

Shane Claiborne, *The Irresistible Revolution*, Zondervan, 2006

Duncan Clark, *The Rough Guide to Ethical Shopping*, Rough Guides, 2004

Christopher Cramer, *Civil War is Not a Stupid Thing*, C. Hurst & Co., 2006

E. Philip Davis, *A confrontation of economic and theological approaches to 'ending poverty' in Africa*, Brunel University Economics and Finance Working Paper No. 07–14, 2007

Department for International Development (DFID), *Preventing Violent Conflict*, Crown Copyright, 2006

Patrick Dixon, *The Truth About AIDS* (4th edn), ACET
    International/OM, 2004

Charles Elliott, *Comfortable Compassion?*, Hodder &
    Stoughton, 1987
David Evans with Kathryn Scherer, *Creating Space for
    Strangers*, IVP, 2004

Ajith Fernando, *After the Tsunami*, RBC Ministries, 2005
Richard Foster, *Celebration of Discipline*, Hodder &
    Stoughton, 1978

Pete Grieg and Dave Roberts, *Red Moon Rising: The Story of
    24-7 Prayer*, Kingsway, 2004
Graham Gordon, *What if I Got Involved? Taking a Stand
    Against Social Injustice*, Paternoster, 2003
Simon Guillebaud, *For What It's Worth*, Monarch, 2006
Holy Bible, Today's New International Version (TNIV),
    Hodder & Stoughton/International Bible Society, 2004

Dewi Hughes with Mathew Bennett, *God of the Poor*, OM,
    1998
Bill Hybels, *Courageous Leadership*, Zondervan, 2002

Intergovernmental Panel on Climate Change, *Fourth
    Assessment report: 'Climate Change 2007'*, IPCC Geneva,
    2007

Patrick Johnstone, *Operation World*, Paternoster Lifestyle,
    2001
James Jones, *Jesus and the Earth*, SPCK, 2003

Tony. Killick, *Aid and the Political Economy of Policy Change*,
    Routledge, 1998

Roy McCloughry, *Taking Action*, Frameworks, 1990

David McIlroy, *A Biblical View of Law and Justice*,
	Paternoster, 2004
Melba Maggay, *Transforming Society*, Regnum, 1994
James Mawdsley, *The Heart Must Break*, Century, 2001
Bryant L. Myers, *Walking with the poor: Principles and
	practices of transformational development*, Orbis, 1999

Rob Parsons, *The Money Secret*, Hodder & Stoughton, 2005

Jeffrey Sachs, *The End of Poverty*, Penguin, 2005
Michael Schluter and David Lee, *The R Factor*, Hodder &
	Stoughton, 1993
Clare Short, *An Honourable Deception*, Free Press, 2004
Ronald Sider, *Rich Christians in an Age of Hunger* (4th
	edition), Hodder & Stoughton, 1997
Tom Sine, *The Mustard Seed Conspiracy*, MARC Europe, 1981
Sir Nicholas Stern, *Stern Review on the Economics of Climate
	Change*, HM Treasury, 2006
John Stott, *Issues Facing Christians Today*, Marshall, Morgan
	and Scott, 1984

Tearfund, *For Tomorrow Too* (3rd edn), Tearfund, 2006
Sarah Tillett (ed.), *Caring for Creation*, The Bible Reading
	Fellowship, 2005
Desmond Tutu, *God Has a Dream*, Rider, 2004

United Nations Millennium Ecosystem Assessment,
	Ecosystems and Human Well-being, Island Press, 2005

Ruth Valerio, *L is for Lifestyle*, IVP, 2004
Paul Vallely, *Bad Samaritans*, Hodder & Stoughton, 1990

Jim Wallis, *Faith Works*, SPCK, 2002
Jim Wallis, *God's Politics*, Harper San Francisco, 2005
Rick Warren, *The Purpose Driven Life*, Zondervan, 2002

Martin Wroe and Malcolm Doney, *The Rough Guide to a Better World*, Rough Guides, 2006

Brother Yun and Paul Hattaway, *The Heavenly Man*, Monarch, 2002

Index

Scripture Index

Notes

Chapter 1: A Call to Action

1.1 The United Nations Millennium Campaign quotes figures of 100 million children out of school, and a cost of $10 billion per year required to achieve Universal Primary Education (see www.millenniumcampaign.org, Goal 2). Euromonitor quotes European ice cream sales of $20.3 billion in 2004 (www.euromonitor.com).

1.2 Figures for 2006 development assistance of $104 billion come from the Development Assistance Committee of the Organization for Economic Co-operation and Development (www.oecd.org/dac). Military expenditure in 2006 was $1,204 billion; information from the Stockholm International Peace Research Institute (SIPRI): www.sipri.org, http://yearbook2007.sipri.org/chap8.

1.3 Bill Hybels, *Courageous Leadership*, Zondervan, 2002.

Chapter 2: Why Should We Get Involved?

2.1 Interview between Bill Hybels and Bono, Willow Creek Pastors' Conference, 2006.

2.2 See *World Development Indicators 2007*, World Bank: www.worldbank.org/data.wdi.

Chapter 3: The Big Issues and How Christians Can Be Different

3.1   Data on child mortality from *The Progress of Nations*, 2000, Unicef: www.unicef.org/pon00/.

3.2   *World Development Indicators*, World Bank, 2005.

3.3   Data for Korea and Zambia from the Globalis interactive world map of the Global Virtual University: http://globalis.gvu.unu.edu. In 1975 South Korea had income per head of $1,310 (in current purchasing power parity prices) while Zambia had $470. Between 1975 and 2003 Korea's income rose to $18,000 while Zambia's rose only to $850, which represents a decline in real terms.

3.4   Data on resources for various disasters is from *World Disasters Report 2006*. (International Federation of Red Cross and Red Crescent Societies, Geneva, 2006).

3.5   Source: World Bank, *World Development Report 2006*.

3.6   World Bank Concept note for HIV/AIDS workshop, Accra, Ghana, January 2004, quoted in *Working Together* (Tearfund, 2006, p. 12), www.tearfund.org/hiv.

3.7   Life expectancy data from World Bank, *World Development Report 2007*. Data on AIDS treatment from www.avert.org/worldstats.

3.8   See www.avert.org/worldstats.

3.9   Sir John Houghton speaking at Tearfund event, Manchester, July 2007.

3.10   Christopher Cramer, *Civil War is Not a Stupid Thing*, C. Hurst & Co., 2006, p. 1.

Chapter 4: What Causes Poverty and How Can It Be Reduced?

4.1   For an interesting analysis of Jeff Sachs' work, and a comparison of his approach with that of Ronald Sider, see E. Philip Davis (2007), 'A confrontation of economic and theological approaches to "ending poverty" in Africa', Brunel

University Economics and Finance Working Paper No. 07–14.

4.2   I am grateful to David McIlroy for this key insight.

4.3   For the full text see the Micah Network website at http://en.micahnetwork.org.

Chapter 5: Who Needs to Do What?

5.1   Such budgetary support is very similar in its effects to debt cancellation.

Appendix 5.1: Does Aid Work?

5.1.1   See, for example, Peter Bauer, *Dissent on Development*, Weidenfeld and Nicolson, 1976.

5.1.2   Summarized in *Assessing Aid*, World Bank, 1998.

5.1.3   See Tony Killick, *Aid and the Political Economy of Policy Change*, Routledge, 1998.

Chapter 8: Action 1: Praying

8.1   Patrick Johnstone, *Operation World*, Paternoster Lifestyle, 2001.

8.2   Heidi Baker quote from her talk at the Elios Church, London, March 2007.

8.3   Brother Yun and Paul Hattaway, *The Heavenly Man*, Monarch, 2002.

Chapter 9: Action 2: Campaigning

9.1   Cited by the Religious Liberty Commission of the World Evangelical Alliance, www.worldevangelicalalliance.com/commissions/rlc/. See report at http://worldevangelical.org/textonly/3persecanalysis.htm.

Chapter 14: Action 7: Living Simply

14.1 Analysis and examples taken from 'Worlds Apart: A call to responsible global tourism' (Tearfund, 2002). This can be found at www.tearfund.org/tilz.

14.2 Source: www.creditaction.org.uk.

Chapter 15: Action 8: Living Sustainably

15.1 See the United Nations Millennium Ecosystem Assessment Report, *Ecosystems and Human Well-being*, Island Press, 2005, www.millenniumassessment.org.

15.2 Sir Nicholas Stern, *Stern Review on the Economics of Climate Change*, HM Treasury, 2006. The report is downloadable from www.hm-treasury.gov.uk.